HOD-CARRIER

Notes of a Laborer on an Unfinished Cathedral

HOD-CARRIER

*Notes of a Laborer
on an Unfinished
Cathedral*

GERALD W. JOHNSON

William Morrow
and Company
New York 1964

By the Same Author

The Man Who Feels Left Behind
The Lunatic Fringe
This American People
Incredible Tale

For Young People

Communism, An American's View
The Government
  The Presidency
  The Supreme Court
  The Congress
A History for Peter
  America is Born
  America Grows Up
  America Moves Forward

Contents

To All to Whom

These Presents May Come

UNTIL THE SPRING OF 1963, HAD I BEEN ASKED I would have said without hesitation that the poetry of Thomas Hardy was so dull as to be virtually unreadable; but then, in Moses Hadas' *Old Wine, New Bottles,* a plea for the humanities, I found a quotation from Hardy that I cannot forget. I still lack the temerity to offer it as great poetry, but it sounds a philosophic note that I heard in youth but did not comprehend until much later, and so it has for me a nostalgic appeal of no small potency. It is the perfect expression of the spirit of a wise man I knew half a century ago, a professor of one of the humanities, English literature, in a small Southern college. I do not think that Old Slick, as he was known to irreverent sophomores, ever cited these particular lines, although he may have done so without causing them to register on young ears; but as I read them in 1903 I could hear in memory the somewhat high, somewhat querulous voice of the old scholar intoning them to young students:

> Sophocles, Plato, Socrates,
>   Gentlemen,
> Pythagoras, Thucydides,
> Herodotus and Homer,—yea,
> Clement, Augustin, Origen
> Burnt brightlier towards their setting-day,
>   Gentlemen.

3

And ye, red-lipped and smooth-browed; list,
  Gentlemen;
Much is there waits you we have missed;
Much lore we leave you worth the knowing,
Much, much has lain outside our ken:
Nay, rush not; time serves; we are going,
  Gentlemen.

To use, reluctantly, the mechanical word of a mechanical-minded generation, the "operative" line in that is "Much lore we leave you worth the knowing." It challenges the good faith of a man who attained a state of relative consciousness before the turn of the century and who therefore cannot be expected to hang around much longer. We are going; that much is incontestable, and it is hardly open to doubt that we can say truthfully to the red-lipped and smooth-browed, "much lore we leave you." The debatable phrase is "worth the knowing." As one of the passing generation I cannot fully share the poet's confidence; I let the line stand, yet I am haunted by a suspicion that a good deal of all that this twentieth century has learned is not worth the knowing, and some of it is definitely, as the doctors say, contraindicated.

For instance, we have learned that sadism perpetrated to its hideous end on six million human beings is quite endurable. Vocally and outwardly we may have protested, but inwardly and silently we adopted George Bernard Shaw's attitude of callousness that would have revolted "Clement, Augustin, Origen." After all, they were Hitler's Jews, not ours, and if he was fool enough to destroy valuable people, it was his folly, not ours. The illusion of the American as Humanitarian went into the gas chamber with those Jews; we know now that he was an *eidolon*, an image, not a reality, and it is doubtful that the knowledge has done us anything but harm.

We have unveiled the processes of atomic fission and fusion. That knowledge one cannot evaluate certainly. On balance, it has thus far been baleful; its chief effect has been to supplant the American as Humanitarian with another *eidolon*, the American as the Besom of Destruction. There are, however, indications, faint but undeniable, that in the course of time the balance may be reversed. The atomic piles have already produced isotopes of some medical and other scientific value and may eventually become efficient sources of industrial power; so that lore, not worth the knowing to my generation, may yet be of great profit to the red-lipped and smooth-browed. One cannot say.

One may and must say, however, that observation of the course of events throughout the twentieth century thus far lends force to what Karl Jaspers told the University of Basle at its quincentenary:

> Whoever has had the exerience of knowledge is acquainted with the appeal of the *sapere audi*, the appeal to the courage not to stop. Having the will to know is not a harmless business. The consequences of knowledge are not within sight. The beginning of modern science is also the beginning of a calamity.*

This is, of course, rank heresy to one whose early schooling was in the Socratic tradition, holding that the basis of all evil is ignorance. But before Jaspers spoke, the former blithe certainty that the pursuit of knowledge is the matrix of virtue had taken a severe battering from events of the first half of the twentieth century; and where it has survived at all, it has survived forspent and bedraggled. Yet the beating that shattered the certainty that all knowledge is good had little effect on the *sapere audi*, which is, the theologians assure us, the legacy of Adam, who had the audacity to taste the fruit of the tree of knowledge of good and evil, bequeath-

Truth and Science, address by Karl Jaspers at the 500th anniversary of the University of Basle. Translated in the *Graduate Journal* of the University of Texas (Spring, 1962).

ing that recklessness and its attendant damnation to all his descendants. Yet, again according to the theologians, God seems to have changed His mind; for when Solomon asked that very thing, "an understanding heart to discern between good and bad," the demand so pleased the Lord that He granted the young king what he had not asked—riches, and honor, and the lives of his enemies.

It would appear, then, that red-lipped and smooth-browed gentlemen should be instructed by us of the passing generation that the audacity to know is the fount, the original source of sin, death, hell, the grave, wisdom, honor, riches, and victory. What good that knowledge will do them, the gentlemen must figure for themselves; we who are going can say only that it is part of the much that has lain outside our ken.

Jaspers, convinced that *sapere audi,* the daring to be informed, is dangerous business, yet acknowledged that its appeal is irresistible; what, then, would he have said of *docere audi,* the daring to teach? It is obviously far more dangerous, but its appeal has been powerful enough to bind Karl Jaspers all his life, as it bound Socrates to the rejection of life, when the choice was between life and teaching.

Nor is it self-centered. If the complex of manners, customs, and activities that we describe vaguely as Western civilization has a chance to postpone, for any considerable length of time, the dissolution that has overtaken all its predecessors, it owes that chance to the spreading knowledge of the methods by which earlier civilizations have committed suicide. This possession—written history partially disentangled from mythology—was available to no civilization earlier than ours, and it is reasonable to assume that it will make a difference.

Certainly the Greeks had Herodotus and Thucydides, the Romans Tacitus and Livy, with dozens of lesser people writing Greek and Latin. But Gibbon and Mommsen, with their like, do not constitute the intellectual discipline called modern history; archaeology, philology, and a dozen other sciences with, above all, the art of printing are essential components of it, its extensions, vertically into the past and horizontally into all classes of society.

The immense enlargement of its range has established history as a social force in modern times, as it was not in any earlier civilization. It is a reasonable assumption that any new force will have an unprecedented effect. The thrust may be in the direction of the disintegration of society; but it may be toward its cohesion. It is too early to tell, for if modern history began with Voltaire, Gibbon, and Ranke, it is roughly coeval with the American republic, and what use we may make of "the register of the crimes, follies and misfortunes of mankind" remains to be seen.

One may hope, though, that its effect will be to enable us to avoid some of the more egregious follies that have led to the destruction of nations and civilizations in the past. It is a wavering hope, for thus far the record of the struggle with human folly parallels the myth of Hercules and the Hydra—when one imbecility is cut off, two new ones promptly replace it. The unitary dictatorship of Caesar is supplanted by pluralistic kings, and they by the multifarious dictatorship of the proletariat; the pike gives way to gunpowder and lead, they to atomic fission, lethal gas, and napalm. Yet, though wavering, it is the only hope, therefore to be cherished.

History exists because men in increasing numbers, learned men and ignorant, heroes and poltroons, rogues and worthies, have made records of what they have seen and heard. All of them are inaccurate in part, yet few are false altogether; and, as Woodrow Wilson said he gained an approximation of the truth about Mexico by "balancing lies," so the historian, supplied with misinformation by the ton, extracts golden truth by the ounce. Supplying the ore is but menial labor, yet not dishonorable; men who have lived in crucial times owe apologies to none for setting down what they think they have learned. Most of it will be wrong, but the residuum of accuracy constitutes the building blocks of history.

Many years ago I stood in the nave at Chartres, entranced by the wrong thing, the rose window. We have the authority of Henry Adams for it that the blue in the lancets is the great glory of the cathedral, superior to any of the glass in the rose; which may be true, but it was the blaze of the great circle that filled me with wonder and awe as I thought of what artists they were who designed, and what craftsmen who executed, that marvel. To dream of rivaling the work of such men would be sheer lunacy. Not until afterward did I remember that the window owes part of its effect, not to its artistry, but to its position. At eye level it would lose heavily; but hoist toward the firmament, it became supernatural.

Its position, of course, it owes to the masonry supporting and surrounding it, and the masonry was put there, not by artists, but by artisans, common workmen, no more inspired than I am, but indispensable.

Adams, however, bases much of his philosophy of history on the theory that, although workmen, they were not common. They were, indeed, so uncommon that they furnish one of the chief supports of his contrast of thirteenth-century unity with nineteenth-century diversity. He despaired of the recovery of their quality and thought that its loss sealed the doom of the Western world.

The building of Chartres took almost the whole of two centuries, so that no man who saw its foundations laid lived to see the completed work; and as the original design was altered repeatedly, none could have imagined what it would eventually be. The masons who laid the stones beneath and around the rose window probably never saw it in place. But in Henry Adams' opinion that mattered little to them; the lowliest hod-carrier among them believed that he was building to the glory of God and the salvation of his own soul; therefore the unseen and unimagined outcome could not be other than magnificent.

The factual truth of their belief is immaterial. The point is that it lent to the drudgery of shaping and placing stones a dignity that lifted it, in Hannah Arendt's subtle distinction, from the level of labor to that of work. A painted house represents labor only, but a painted landscape is a work.

Therein, it seems to me, is the germ of a philosophy of history that might supply an answer to the disconcerting question posed by *Life* a year or two before these lines were written. What, the magazine asked of seven pundits, should be our national purpose? It was disconcerting because the seven struggled with it to no persuasive conclusion, or, to be exact, to seven contradictory conclusions. None had the hardihood to make the obviously appropriate answer, which is: How the hell should we know?

To be sure, one might quote the inscription on the Supreme Court building "Equal Justice under law," or the finale of the preamble to the Constitution, "and secure the blessings of liberty to ourselves and our posterity," but each is a *petitio principii*, a begging of the question, because each presupposes that one knows what liberty, justice, and law are, which knowledge is revealed to no man.

The experience of more than seventy years has given me as little knowledge of the ultimate destiny of the United States as a hod-carrier of Chartres in the year 1201 had of the final appearance of the cathedral. Yet that experience has brought me much lore, some part of it, perhaps, worth the knowing, and much of it amusing, appalling, or humiliating. More to my present purpose, it has brought me a firm conviction that on balance it is good to have been an American citizen in the twentieth century. If a man has indeed found, or thinks he has found, satisfactions that overcompensate for the frustrations in having lived and labored in times like these on a task like this, he ought to say so; for if he offers himself as a target to the scornful, yet he may serve the purpose that Voltaire attributed to the English in shooting one admiral—"to encourage the others."

So, now that the sound of Time's winged chariot hurrying near resolves into the admonition, "If you have anything to say, man, say it now, for permanent silence is at hand," I have taken heed.

I have said.

On the Embarrassment

Occasioned by Unsolicited Kisses

IN THE SPRING OF 1963 THE SENIOR SENATOR from California, the Hon. Thomas H. Kuchel, hit the ceiling, thereby becoming, of course, front-page, top-of-column news, for a raving Senator is ever the reporters' pride and joy. It is inexact to say that the Californian was hoist by his own petard, although it was one engineered by members, at least titular members, of his own party. Mr. Kuchel, a Republican, was sprung by the activities of those persons who professed to have found a Communist agent in Dwight D. Eisenhower, a parlor pink in Richard M. Nixon, and obedience to a command from Moscow in the school segregation decision of a unanimous Supreme Court. These persons—typified by, but not confined to, the John Birch Society—for the most part profess to be Republicans, of the right wing to be sure, but still Republicans.

This was the goad that pricked the California Senator into fury. He made the point, and supported it with notable plausibility, that they are not Republicans but a terrorist group. True, up to the time of the Senator's speech they had operated exclusively with psychological explosives rather than with "villainous saltpetre," but the effect, according to Mr. Kuchel, is none the less shattering; and it made him apprehensive of the future of the republic.

It is hardly to be denied that his anxiety was based upon

reason. Since no country ever ran itself or ever will, it follows
that the national future always hangs upon the quality of
the individuals in whom the people repose their confidence.
If the fact that a man has brain power enough to move him
to get in out of the rain is, as the terrorists imply, proof
positive that he is a Communist or a Communist dupe, it is
a necessary inference that, as anti-Communists, we must
entrust the conduct of public affairs to the completely brain-
less. Then when those who advocate this course insist that
they are Republicans, and the only simon-pure, 24-carat
Republicans, acute embarrassment is caused those Republicans who retain faith in government by intelligence. But
what can they do? Little, it appears, but squirm.

Senator Kuchel was disturbed by this situation. So, indeed,
are some others. The Declaration of Independence asserts
the right of the people to choose the form of government
that "to them shall seem most likely to effect their Safety
and Happiness." The choice is restricted only by the opinion
of the people; yet to persons of like mind with the Senator,
imbecile leadership seems unlikely, highly unlikely, to effect
anybody's safety and happiness. Nevertheless, the possibility
that it may be the people's choice takes on the look of a
probability when the wholesalers of terror are doing a thriving business.

At such moments a long memory, often an affliction, becomes consolatory. A citizen of the United States who has
endured in a state of partial awareness for more than sixty
years has this advantage over youth: whatever damfool
thing comes up, he has seen the like before and has observed
that in the long run it didn't amount to much. The development that agitated Senator Kuchel in 1963 is a case in point.
It was the effectiveness, or what he considered the effectiveness, of the work of the terrorists. In this the Senator obviously descried evidence of some deterioration in the

national character; but to an older American it is merely evidence of the continuing prevalence of Dr. Wirt.

It was in 1934 that Dr. William Albert Wirt, already a pedagogue of some fame, achieved a sudden political notoriety that jarred to their heels such equivalents of Senator Kuchel as then flourished. He laid before Congress information that Franklin D. Roosevelt, who had been President of the United States for about a year, was not the leader of a reform movement, as was generally supposed, but was merely a stopgap, comparable to the Russian who held power briefly between the abdication of Czar Nicholas Romanoff and the advent of Dictator Nicholas Lenin.

But in measure as the scale of events had enlarged between 1917 and 1934, it might be assumed that Roosevelt, obviously a bigger man than Kerensky, would presently be ejected to make room for a successor correspondingly bigger than Lenin, one of a redness that would make Lenin's hue a pale flesh tint by comparison. This information, Dr. Wirt averred, he had from authorities so close to the center of power as to be unimpeachable.

The epidemic of gooseflesh raised by this pronouncement spread from Sandy Hook to the Golden Gate. Its dimensions were such as to bring the ordinarily imperturbable Edmund Wilson onto the scene as an investigator. His report to *Scribner's*, published in August, 1934, was doubtless factually correct, but I, for one, have never believed that it got at the truth.

The facts as reported by Wilson were that Dr. Wirt, on a business trip to Washington, was entertained at dinner by a former associate who then held a position in a government department. The other guests were three or four minor officials, all of them young and enthusiastic New Dealers. The Doctor seized the occasion to promulgate his views on fiscal policy, including certain theories of monetary reform that he was urging at the time. The evening turned into a monologue of four hours' duration. It was the testimony of the witnesses that nobody mentioned the name of Kerensky; nobody mentioned anything else very much, for the Doctor held the floor and brooked no interruption.

This Wilson chronicled, obviously in good faith, and there is no reason to doubt that it is literal truth; but that it was the effective truth I, for one, will never believe. It is simply not congruent with the spirit of the early New Deal, and I doubt that any social event in Washington in that period was entirely unaffected by the spirit of the time. It was blithe, adventurous, and intellectually alive even to excess. In 1934 Washington was hell on solemn asses, and to assume that Dr. Wirt escaped unscathed strains credulity beyond the breaking point.

I shall go to the grave believing that he did have authority for his statement and that he did regard it as unimpeachable. He was trapped by a constiutional inability to comprehend sarcasm. The probability, so great as to approximate mathematical certainty, is that by the time the monologue was well into its third hour some young New Dealer, bored beyond endurance, interjected a comment so obviously satirical as to pass unnoticed by the rest, and so forgotten, but which was swallowed at a gulp by the Doctor.

The reader, who is certainly rational or he would not be reading these lines, may be tempted to reject this as incredible; but it is a hasty judgment that he will retract after brief consideration. He has only to ask himself: Why was Dr. Wirt there at all? The answer, common knowledge at the time, excited no startled comment; Dr. Wirt was there to advise the government on its monetary problems, which were then very serious.

The fact that this occasioned no astonishment reveals, on analysis, one of the chief fascinations of life in the United

States during the first sixty years of the twentieth century. It alone might persuade one to echo Adlai Stevenson's remark that he is glad to have lived at this time; for it touches a folk belief intensely American and florid enough to match anything in any of Frazer's twelve volumes.

Dr. Wirt in Washington was a reiteration of faith in an American myth noted by nearly all observers, but most aptly named by Walter Lippmann as "the myth of the omnicompetent citizen." From Tocqueville through Bryce down to Maurois and Brogan, visitors from other countries have been struck by the curious belief of Americans that excellence is not so much an acquired character as a status, a level in the psychic hierarchy comparable to the peerage in the British social hierarchy. Even as the British hold that if a man is a duke he is totally a duke and cannot be other than ducal, so Americans hold that if a man is able he is totally able, and it is not admissible that the same man can philosophize on one subject and merely bray on another. If experience shows us that it is possible, so much the worse for experience.

Hence if one appeared among us demonstrating such superlative ability at the painting of barber poles that never in recorded history had another lived who could approach him as a painter of barber poles, it is a moral certainty that in the spring of the next election year someone would propose the painter for President of the United States. Have we not seen advocates of Henry Ford, J. Edgar Hoover, and Will Rogers for the White House?

Now Dr. Wirt in early and middle life had been a dominie of note, not merely agile enough in body to dodge spitballs and fragments of chalk, but also agile enough in mind to devise a system of shifting pupils in such wise as to increase the operational capacity of schoolhouses impressively—he claimed by 40 per cent—and to speed up the educational process by 20 per cent. This system, first applied in the steel-making town of Gary, Indiana, and known to educationists as the Gary Plan, seems to have been an adaptation of assembly-line technique to the tutorial process.

The Gary Plan so elevated its inventor in the esteem of his fellow citizens that few saw any incongruity in his appearance at Washington to advise Treasury officials on monetary theory and fiscal policy. If a rose is a rose is a rose, then surely a wizard is a wizard is a wizard, and butter must be good for the works of a watch, provided it is the very best butter. A genius capable of adapting mass production to scholarship ought to have no trouble at all with a relatively simple problem, such as stabilization of the currency.

As for the young New Dealers who apparently stuffed the Doctor with chaff, one may say of them as of Hamlet's players, "They do but jest; poison in jest; no offence i' the world." Presumably they were of one mind with Senator Kuchel; they could not understand how such stuff could be swallowed by any rational man. It did not occur to them that he would accept it avidly; like the Senator, they fell into the common error of assuming that fear is consistently unpleasant, therefore avoided by all but the abnormal.

But as a matter of fact the discomfort of fear is relative. Boredom is a worse affliction. When people's lives are sufficiently dull they may invite fear as a break in the monotony. If nothing else scares them, they will scare themselves. Why else does the world delight in ghost stories? Unwittingly, no doubt, but obviously, Dr. Wirt came to Washington determined to be scared, and the young New Dealers only saved him the trouble of devising means to scare himself.

Senator Kuchel's agitation might have persisted, but hardly with the same intensity, if he had borne this fact in mind. The people of the extreme right experience a delicious horror in discovering in Eisenhower a Communist dupe, and in the Chief Justice a commissar in disguise. Shock relieves the tedium of an otherwise empty existence and so is not entirely unwelcome.

Suppose, though, that such people become so numerous as to constitute a majority able to take over the government? Was not the Senator justified in assuming that such an event would signalize the end of the republic as we have known it? That hardly admits of a doubt; but two comments on the possibility would seem to be relevant. The first is that it is remote; a large proportion of vacuous minds conjure up their bugaboos outside the field of politics. The second is: Who wants the republic as we know it to survive indefinitely?

Anti-intellectualism has tried often enough to take over, and sometimes its efforts have been strong enough to alarm the judicious. When the late Joseph McCarthy was raging, some highly intelligent men were half persuaded, momentarily, that he had won over a majority. It was an illusion. The event proved that his real followers, as distinguished from the gaping bystanders, had never been numerically strong; it was vocally that they were overwhelming.

This has been true of earlier aberrations comparable to McCarthyism back to the Know-Nothings and the Anti-Masons of the early nineteenth century. There is reason to believe that Huey Long came much closer than McCarthy to winning a national majority, but even the Kingfish fell far short of the mark. True, there must be a first time for everything, and the eventual appearance of an American Cleon is possible. But that it is fairly distant seems likely because it is contingent on one or both of two developments, either of which must be a rather long process. Some master demagogue may sweep the country, but not until the American people have slipped back from their present level of political maturity, or until the art of demagoguery has been perfected to a degree beyond the capacity of McCarthy, Long, or any other practitioner hitherto known. Or both.

Against this one must balance the possibility that our level of political maturity, instead of sinking, may rise, in which case success of the demagogue would tend to become less and less probable. I am persuaded that this has been the tendency since the adoption of the Constitution. It is admittedly a guess, and some formidable authorities have guessed the contrary—the Adams brothers, for instance, and even Justice Holmes in moments of exceptional acerbity. But the great men were guessing, too, and the latest guesser has the advantage over all predecessors that with each passing year there is more evidence on which to base a guess. Hence there is no logical necessity that some future McCarthy or Long will take over the White House; and it may be plausibly argued that the trend is in the direction of making it less probable every year.

But the survival of the republic as we have known it is a proposition of a different order. The word "survive" as applied to any part except the name of the United States of America is a semantic sin. What is left of the government over which George Washington presided is hardly visible to the naked eye. The United States has not survived, it has evolved—a completely different concept. That its evolution will continue seems to me as near to mathematical certainty as any political prediction can come.

Theoretically, it might evolve into a monstrosity comparable to the saurians of the Mesozoic, whose sheer dimensions guaranteed their extinction in a changing environment; or it may evolve into something admirable but indescribable because it has no historical referent. Neither outcome can be precisely described as survival. When my father built his house in Thomasville, North Carolina, there was before it a sapling no taller than a schoolboy. Sixty years later the spot is occupied by a large hickory tree, an ornament to the property but emphatically not a sapling. The sapling is not there, although it never died; no more is the republic that existed when Washington was inaugurated as its first President existent now; and it is a reasonable assumption that the republic I know will not be existent when my youngest grandson is as old as I am now.

Obviously, living men fall into two classifications as they regard this prospect gloomily or serenely. Since nobody lacking the gift of prophecy can by any process of thought determine which is the more probable outcome, the class into which one falls, optimist or pessimist, is presumably a matter of temperament. Yet who will admit it? All of us believe implicitly and usually explicitly that, whatever may be true of others, our attitude is determined by logical cogitation. Hence philosophy.

It seems that Bertrand Russell, as age crept upon him, grew more rather than less cheerful. He always was contrary. For instance, at eighty-plus he said, "We are equal to all that we can understand." I feel sure that at sixty he would have said, "We are equal to no more than we can understand," and at forty, "We are equal only to what we can understand, which is precious little." Since the quantity of truth that each of these sayings would assay is indeterminate, I choose to adhere to his lordship in his eighties and, on the theory that we are equal to all that we can understand, hazard the prediction that this nation will be equal to more and more as understanding widens with the passage of the generations. Perhaps it will eventually be equal to what Kant called the greatest task facing humanity, to wit, creation of civic order based on justice rather than on force.

But to date it has never been equal to that task, perhaps because the task has never been understood. I am hopeful, therefore, that the United States as I know it will not survive through an indefinite future. It is not that good. In the assurance that it will evolve I can cheerfully face the possibility that it might evolve monstrously, seeing that it is equally possible that it may evolve beautifully, whereas mere survival would mean no change. If the time had come when we could be assured that the United States will never be appreciably better than it is now, a man of sense should attempt to make a reservation in the next space capsule; for all that makes it tolerable would be extracted from terrestrial existence.

I do not flatter myself that this kind of rationalizing will do much to relieve Senator Kuchel's distress at finding himself in intimate, unwanted contact with political grotesques; but it may help if he can be assured that his personal discomfort is not necessarily the prelude to national disaster. Which is really about all that can be done for a man luckless enough to be kissed by the intellectually slobbery.

On Abstract Justice
as a Psychic Vitamin

IN THE SPRING OF 1963 RACE RELATIONS IN THIS
country were subjected to two severe shocks resulting from
explosions in Birmingham and Norman Podhoretz. The Birmingham disturbance was physical, involving rioting in the
streets. The Podhoretz affair was psychic, but its repercus-
sions were so extensive that it may prove to have more historical significance than the rioting.

For at the moment when he blew up, Mr. Podhoretz stood
very near the top among intellectuals, among Jews, and
among liberals. He edited *Commentary*, the brilliant review
sponsored, but not censored, by the American Jewish Committee, and politically he stood somewhat left of center,
although short of the Socialist, not to mention the Communist position. Such was the man who, in a carefully considered essay in the February issue of his magazine, confessed that he just doesn't like Negroes.

The fact is proof to Mr. Podhoretz that he is a sick man, and
his essay is an endeavor to account for this psychopathic
condition. Parts of it he traces to traumatic experiences in
childhood, when he was subjected to oppression and perse-
cution at the hands of the Negro boys in his neighborhood;
but he is not entirely satisfied with that explanation. He
suspects the presence of some morbidity lying below the
reach of the most penetrating analysis; and it fills him with
foreboding.

It will hardly assuage his fears to be told that a diametrically opposite experience may lead to the identical result. My own childhood was in every superficial aspect save one directly opposed to that of Mr. Podhoretz—rural, not urban; privileged, not suppressed; racially and religiously dominant, not dominated. As far as indoctrination went, it was anti-racist; when I first heard the word "nigger" I was informed, with the utmost emphasis, that it was an obscenity, and if I were heard uttering it I was promised a switching laid on with vigor. Only at ten or twelve did I discover, with genuine astonishment, that there existed a class of white boys who regarded "rocking (i.e., stoning) niggers" as a legitimate pastime; but I was informed that it was a very low class and a disgrace to the white race. Swimming and fishing with colored boys of my own age was a matter of course, while disrespect toward or disobedience of Aunt Penny, the nursemaid, was visited with condign punishment.

Poverty seems to have been the sole point at which Mr. Podhoretz's experience and mine ran parallel, and I am not sure of that, for poverty is relative. Since nobody, white or black, in my neighborhood gained much more than bare subsistence from his labor, who was poor?

In sum, I can remember no emotional experience connected with racism that could account for a genuine trauma; but I cannot deny some infection with the sickness that Mr. Podhoretz described. But is it an infection? Is not the analogy rather with scurvy, a deficiency disease? Mr. Podhoretz thinks so. He attributes his malaise to lack of love, an emotional vitamin essential to psychological health. The difficulty is that his system seems unable to assimilate love of Negroes, hence in 1963 he despaired so vociferously as to scandalize a large proportion of his readers.

It may be, though, that the analogy can be pressed a little further without reduction to absurdity, and if so, utter despair is not justified. Vitamins are not assimilable by every person in every form, but due allowance for idiosyncratic differences will usually overcome the trouble. Granting that a deficiency of love is the cause of our morbid state, it is arguable that we ought to take the corrective dosage in the form of love of justice rather than in the form of love of any minority alien to us, whether ethnically, theologically, or politically.

I am not prepared to advance this as a panacea, but I do contend that it is effective against acute seizures, such as the Birmingham riots. In the absence of any known cure, anything that will bring the malady under control, even partially, is a boon; for once it is under control we may pursue the search for a cure with scientific detachment rather than frantically.

Some purists will reject this suggestion out of hand. In the same review, a few months after Mr. Podhoretz's confession, another writer, Mr. Hans Morgenthau, the Chicago savant, argued powerfully against the possibility of the attainment of justice. To do justly, said Mr. Morgenthau, three qualifications are essential: the will, the means, and the knowledge. The will to administer equal and exact justice, he continued, is confined to an ethically superior minority; the means of working justice are available only to a minority of that minority; and knowledge of what is just varies so widely from case to case that nobody possesses it in full. Hence the administration of justice in this world is an unattainable ideal.

Be that as it may, the fact that an ideal is unattainable in no way negates its existence. On the contrary, it is a condition of its persistence as an ideal; for attained, it is no longer an ideal but an achievement. Yet love of the unattainable is within our reach, or philosophy is belied by its very name. It is certainly arguable, therefore, that love of justice may be attainable even by persons who find the love of Negroes beyond their emotional capacity.

A characteristically arrogant pronunciamento of John Randolph of Roanoke, "I am an aristocrat; I love justice and hate equality," has been widely accepted as corroborative evidence that old John was insane. But the logical fallacy in the statement is not apparent unless one identifies justice with equality, which is certainly fallacious. To regard an honest man and a thief as equals in an absurdity; and hatred of equality is historically characteristic of aristocrats.

The stumbling block, as far as most of us are concerned, is the universality of the concept of justice. In theory it applies to all men, in all circumstances, at all times, everywhere. It can be grasped, therefore, only by the universal mind, which, if it exists at all, is certainly superhuman. Accordingly, the love of justice will inevitably betray us into the commission of unjust acts on account of our lack of comprehension of what is just. Its recommendation is not that it will always save us from acting unjustly, but that it will occasionally impel us to act justly, while its absence furnishes no impulsion at all. It has, therefore, merit—slight, it may be, but definite—and the important point is that it is attainable.

"I have but one lamp by which my feet are guided, and that is the lamp of experience," proclaimed Patrick Henry. "I know of no way of judging the future but by the past." Quite so; but Henry was making an *ex parte* plea, in which it would have been irrelevant to mention that the lamp is an extremely dim one, assuring highly erratic judgment of the future. This is a condition all but insufferable to logical minds, but it exists, and it accounts for the aberrance of prophecy.

Mr. Podhoretz, for example, looking into history, finds no instance in which disparate races have occupied the same

area on terms of equality over a long period. The only relation in which widely different races have coexisted on the
same ground for a considerable number of centuries is the
relation of master and servant. In the past, any other relation
has invariably ended either in extinction or in amalgamation.
Ethnically, there is no difference, since in either case the
dominated race vanishes.

Following Patrick Henry, but perhaps following him much
too faithfully, Mr. Podhoretz, guided by the lamp of the past,
foresees for the American Negro either extinction or amalgamation. Logically, the prediction is flawless, but there remains a philosophical doubt. It is based on the possibility
that history, especially political history but including anthro-
pological records as well, is an experiment as yet in its very
early stages, and a logical inference is that not all possible
hypotheses have as yet been adumbrated, much less tested.

Extrapolation is an intellectual tool of high value in some,
but not in all, forms of thinking. Mathematicians, statisticians, and engineers could not do without it, and sociologists use it extensively. But in political art—for political
"science" is a contradiction in terms—it is unreliable, and its
failure in that field may lead to fantastic error.

The classical example is that of Karl Marx, who extra-
polated into the indefinite future the economic theory prevalent in the early nineteenth century. But it did not extend
so far, and when it ran out his predictions were left with no
basis. Before he died he was being refuted, not by logicians,
but by events, and less than twenty years after his death his
whole prophetic structure was in a state of collapse. His
titular followers in Russia have been going in a direction
opposite to his ever since the repudiation of Lenin's New
Economic Policy. Yet Marx was a keen and assiduous observer with an intellect that towered even among such contemporaries as Darwin, Galton, and Gauss. His error was

technical, which is to say avoidable; it was choice of the wrong tool for the operation he had in mind.

As regards the ultimate fate of the American Negro, no more than Mr. Podhoretz can I see a third eventuation between extinction and amalgamation. But I am certain that there are vast areas of the possible utterly beyond my conception; so why reject the hypothesis that there are areas beyond the comprehension of any contemporary? In his own field, any scientist or philosopher is my intellectual superior; but it is not arrogance to assume that there may be fields in which we are exactly equal—equal in total ignorance.

In 1867, date of publication of the first volume of *Das Kapital*, Marx made the mistake of taking for permanent certain obvious, but not obviously evanescent, economic trends. He perceived, and expounded with remarkable clarity, the logical outcome of those trends. But even before he died in 1883 some of them were beginning to be reversed, and by the time of the First World War most of them had changed direction, at least in the United States. Thus Marx's logical perception became completely illogical, producing the political and philosophical monstrosity of totalitarianism, as un-Marxian a form of government as ever was known.

In 1963 Mr. Podhoretz and I had, or thought we had, some idea of what the typical white American is like. We also had mental images, perhaps 10 per cent correct, of what the black, the yellow, and the red Americans are like. But the truth that we possessed related, to adopt an auctioneer's term, to the American "as is." I submit that neither of us had, or could have, the faintest conception of what the American of any color will be psychologically, and especially emotionally, ten generations hence. Under present conditions the probability is that it will take five to ten generations to effect either amalgamation or extinction. In the case of a minority numbering twenty millions, ten generations would seem to

be a conservative guess. Therefore Mr. Podhoretz and I had
in 1963 no firm basis for any prediction whatever, simply
because the forces involved will be operative far beyond the
predictable future.

This is, however, no excuse for either action or inaction.
It is simply no excuse. For our generation the twin horrors
of extinction and amalgamation—to the Negro a single
horror, since amalgamation is a form of extinction—are
neither true nor false. They are irrelevant. To base any current policy on conditions that we suppose will exist two or
three centuries hence is irrational. Furthermore, it is insolent.
It presupposes our possession of a wisdom that exceeds not
only any acquired by our forefathers, but also any that posterity can possibly acquire. It is to proclaim that we—you
and I and Joe Doakes down the street—represent the acme,
the highest pinnacle of human achievement; all before us
was laborious ascent; all after us must be decline.

In ancient times the Greeks coined a word, *hubris*, to de-
note a pride so excessive as to outrage even the Olympians,
who visited it with destruction. But the assumption that we
who are living now are wise enough to dictate the conduct
of Americans of the twenty-third century makes *hubris*
totally inadequate to describe our shamelessness.

Superficially this may seem to imply that Patrick Henry
was only gabbling and that Podhoretz is an idiot to concern
himself with the *sequelae* of Birmingham. But it is a decep-
tive appearance. The past *is* a lamp unto our feet and a light
upon our path; and race prejudice *is* a problem that concerns you and me and Podhoretz. The difficulty is our tendency to forget that the past is our guide in the sense that
Polaris guides the mariner whose object is to reach the Line;
as long as he turns his back upon it, he knows that he is on
a true course.

The Constitution of the United States, for instance, is no

more a government than the Pole Star is a voyage. It is
simply a point of reference by which the people who are
actually making the voyage—a constantly shifting crew, but
at the moment including you and me and Podhoretz—may
set the course. It is commonly asserted that the Constitution
itself is unstable in that it has been amended twenty-three
times, but that is an exaggeration. To all practical intents,
the first ten amendments, adopted in one package, are parts
of the original document. Of the remaining thirteen, the
Eighteenth was admittedly a mistake which the Twenty-first
corrects, so they cancel out, leaving eleven. Three of these,
the Thirteenth, Fourteenth, and Fifteenth, were designed to
effect a single change in our system, the abolition of slavery.
The Sixteenth (income tax) merely restored to the government a taxing power that it had exercised for eighteen years
before a decision of the Supreme Court took it away; the
amendment, therefore, did not alter the Constitution, it
merely reversed the Supreme Court. The Twentieth changes
the date of the inauguration of the President, but not the
Constitution; nor is it changed by the Twenty-third, giving
votes to residents of the District of Columbia.

The twenty-three amendments, then, represent only six
material changes in the scheme of government devised by
the writers of the Constitution. They are the exemption of
states from suits by private individuals (XI), the emascula-
tion of the Electoral College (XII), the abolition of slavery
(XIII, XIV, XV), direct election of Senators (XVII), votes
for women (XIX), and the third-term restriction (XXII).
Eventually the real changes will be reduced to five, for the
Twenty-second Amendment will go the way of the
Eighteenth once the people realize that inclusion of an explosion of impotent spite against a dead man insulted the
dignity of the organic law even more than did inclusion of
the sumptuary legislation in the Eighteenth.

The fact that their work has been altered in any essential only five times in the course of nearly two hundred years is usually cited as proof of the remarkable foresight of the Founding Fathers; but is it not rather proof of their almost unparalleled modesty? Classical scholars almost to a man, they realized fully that they were called to the task once assigned to Solon (and to Lycurgus, if any), but not for a moment did they display a confidence in their own wisdom comparable to that of Solon.

They contented themselves with sketching an outline of what the government should be, leaving it to their successors to make it what they had outlined. In the preamble they listed the six ideals that government must strive to realize, and in the body of the document they distributed the powers essential to the realization of those ideals. It was the people, not the members of the Convention, who demanded a clear enumeration of the things the government must not undertake to do. The ablest members of the Convention were willing to accept the Bill of Rights, but they hesitated to claim authority to impose, of their own motion, restrictions on the people's government. It was an exercise of self-restraint that at the time had Washington's surrender of his commission as its only precedent.

It has had no sequent, here or elsewhere. Within the twentieth century, and especially in its third quarter, constitutions have proliferated like mushrooms. In the two decades following the Second World War constitutions were the chief product of statecraft throughout the world; and they seemed to be voluminous in inverse ratio to the size of the state they professed to establish. What one might reasonably assume to be the prototype of them all, the Charter of the United Nations, is twice as long as our Constitution and many times as rigid, which indicates a far greater certainty of the correctness of the forms that it creates.

It may be argued, of course, that modesty was at once the strength and the most conspicuous weakness of the statesmen of 1787; it is the secret of the flexibility that has enabled their work to outlast that of any similar group anywhere on earth, and it also accounts for their one grave error. This was their failure to seize the opportunity, as the wisest among them wished to do, to incorporate in the document provision for the eventual extinction of slavery by lawful means. They did provide for the outlawing of the international slave trade, although they had to allow it an additional twenty years. Perhaps it was the utmost possible. After all, Virginia outweighed the other states then as heavily as New York did a century later, and Virginia's veto might have doomed the whole effort. The fact remains, though, that the omission came nearer than anything else to destroying the Union while it was yet relatively an adolescent nation.

At any rate, what they established was a political hypothesis, which has been in process of testing ever since. The results to date are encouraging, but not conclusive. To date we have resolved only one of the apparent inner contradictions that, if real, must force the abandonment of any hypothesis. That one was slavery, which was eliminated at terrific cost, but effectively. A second, with which we are still struggling, is the apparent contradiction of liberty and law; it has not been solved, but neither has it been proved insoluble.

As regards other aspects, the results are better than the Constitution makers anticipated. For instance, it has been demonstrated that commerce and industry can flourish under the governmental system they adopted with trepidation. Religion, or at least ecclesiasticism, which such pessimists as Theodore Dwight considered doomed, has thrived to the extent that in 1963 more than half of the whole population was enrolled formally in some kind of church. The reign of law is more, not less, firmly established than it was in 1787.

Such results are ample warrant for continuing the experiment along the lines indicated by the Constitutional Convention. The Convention listed as second of the six objectives of an ideal government "to establish justice." Members, of course, were knowingly and willfully offering the counsel of perfection. It is safe to say that not a man among them believed that we should ever establish absolute justice, but they did consider it a worthy ideal, which implies acceptance of love of justice as essential to the creation of reasonably good government.

They had no doubt that it was attainable because they, as a group, possessed it. A few years later John Randolph assumed it to be one of the identifying marks of an aristocrat. But it was not universal then, and it is not universal now; nor is there any convincing evidence that it is more widespread today than it was when the Constitution was written.

Which is, in the opinion of this observer, one reason for the anxiety that has harassed thoughtful Americans in the third quarter of the twentieth century. We have made great advances in operating what may be called the mechanics of democracy. Elections, for instance, are conducted with far greater efficiency and, I think—but the point is debatable— with less distortion of the will of the majority than was the case in earlier times. Life, limb, and property are still imperiled, but in most parts of the country they are safer now than they were in 1787—or 1789, if you prefer the date of proclamation of the Constitution to that of its writing. All this represents some advance in mastery of the practice, as distinguished from the theory, of popular government.

But when it comes to liberty, one can speak with no such assurance. The Negro obviously does not enjoy even the qualified liberty of the white American; but his case, although more conspicuous than any other, is far from unique. An Oriental—Japanese, Chinese, East Indian, or Malay—also suffers disabilities based on racial differences, and a Jew is handicapped by his religion—for whatever the original Hebrews may have been, Jews long ago lost any distinctive racial characteristics.

Perhaps this is attributable to a deficiency in love of variant minorities but, applying the principle of Occam's Razor, I prefer the simpler explanation that it indicates a deficiency in love of justice. It was not any overpowering affection for Germans that sent Andrew Hamilton to the defense of John Peter Zenger; but he went. Love of abstract justice was sufficient, in that case, to lay the mudsill of freedom of the press, regardless of Hamilton's general attitude toward Germans in the mass. I believe that it is still an efficient force, and that if it were more widespread among Americans it would guarantee to the Negro every civil right appertaining to the status of first-class American citizenship; and it would do so even though Mr. Norman Podhoretz's affection for the Rev. Dr. Martin Luther King should remain regrettably languid.

 **IV**

On the Judicious Choice of Obsessions

IN THE SPRING OF 1963 THE JUNIOR SENATOR from South Dakota, the Hon. George S. McGovern, fell short, perhaps of hitting the ceiling but certainly made a sudden, sharp ascent in an article published by the *New York Times Sunday Magazine* and sufficiently described by its title: "Is Castro an Obsession with Us?"

The Senator's answer, as you might expect, was emphatically in the affirmative, in which, it seems to me, he was right; but the Senator regarded the fact as deplorable, in which I presume to doubt that he was entirely right. Any national obsession is theoretically bad, but if, as our history suggests, we must have one, obsession with Castro was probably less harmful than some to which we have fallen victim in the past—with freemasonry, for example, with prohibition, with McCarthyism.

For Castro as the national jinx had the advantages, from our standpoint, first, of being a foreigner, second, of being a real, not a putative, Communist, and, third, of being close at hand. In 1963 we were seeing Castro, not indeed clearly, but more clearly than we could see either Khrushchev or Mao Tse-tung, because he was nearer and yet not obscured by the red haze of emotion created by suspicion of treason. As a foreigner, Castro owed no allegiance to the United States, so there was no question of betrayal to obscure the picture.

39

However, for at least a minority of Americans, vision was clearer for another reason. Wilson's method of getting at truth by balancing lies was becoming operative because many Americans were beginning to realize that, as touching Castro, the thundering lies of Moscow could be approximately balanced by the thundering lies of Washington, and *vice versa*. The resultant would bear enough resemblance to truth to serve as a working hypothesis.

As this realization percolated into their minds, realistic Americans found reason to hope that our obsession with Castro, which was an intensified variant of our earlier obsession with Moscow, might eventually serve a useful purpose. Realists perceived that the Castro affair was beginning to make the United States look ridiculous, and discovery that he is looking like a fool has always been the shock treatment most effective in bringing Uncle Sam back to relative sanity.

The theory that Castro ever was a military threat to this country must rest upon the pessimistic assumption that our military informants, in describing our potential, have been lying to us even more recklessly than they lied during the early phases of the Bay of Pigs operation. On the doubtful theory that his Russian master had supplied Castro with means to blast Miami off the face of Florida, and the assumption that the event would constitute an injury to the United States, it would not be a mortal blow; while if the Pentagon has given us even half the truth, the firepower—of the fleet, of the air force, and of the missile-launching bases, without either infantry or field artillery—that the United States could concentrate on the island is enough speedily to reduce Cuba to a denuded rock, sizzling with radioactivity that might render it uninhabitable for a thousand years.

But there are such things as non-military threats, and Castro was one. This fact was known, of course, to all literate Americans long before 1963, in the sense that they had read it and heard it a thousand times and had not consciously dissented; but they had not assimilated it, they had not incorporated it among the established premises from which their conscious thinking starts. There were too many psychological blocks in the way, the most formidable being the view of Americanism that has prevailed in recent years, especially since 1945. That view is close, too close for comfort, to the delusion of the Master Race, the *Herrenvolk*, that led to the downfall of Germany.

To be sure, none but the lunatic fringe of Americans ever admitted, even to themselves—especially to themselves—that they cherished any such doctrine; but it is badly exposed in action in Hundred Percentism. To admit that Castro or any other alien may be so intelligent that he can actually outsmart a native-born, white, Protestant American bears the frightening implication that a judicious admixture of something else might produce an alloy stronger than the pure metal. This would be tantamount to an admission that Americanism might be improved by the addition of, say, 10 per cent cosmopolitanism; and the admission would cause the whole structure of Hundred Percentism to totter.

Regrettable it may be, but it is certain that the facts support the monstrous suggestion. Throughout history the really hard babies have seldom been Hundred Percenters. Alexander the Great was a Macedonian, not a Greek, Napoleon a Corsican, Hitler an Austrian, Stalin a Georgian. Even our own George Washington was born and bred an English country gentleman. Among the very great American statesmen, only Lincoln and Andrew Jackson can be truthfully described as purely native products.

It is not beyond conjecture, therefore, that this Castro may have had in him from the start an element of toughness against which our military strength is helpless. Even so, it does not necessarily follow that this possibility must drive

the native American into a state of psychological shock. It
need not even shatter his faith in his own essential superiority. His way of escape is simply to realize that his superiority, however evident to himself, is still in process of
demonstration to the rest of the world.

Yet if this realization need not destroy the American's
faith in himself, it must force a very profound change in his
attitude toward the rest of the world. If other nations have
not yet seen the excellence of the American system, they
must be made to see it. This is bound to lead to some hard,
and probably confused and bitter, thinking about methods of
persuasion; for even the thickest-skulled Hundred Percenter
knows that you do not acquire a man's affection and esteem
by kicking him in the teeth.

How much time it will take for this idea to permeate the
electorate far enough to produce a political effect is anybody's guess, but there is no shadow of doubt that Castro
has speeded up the process. He came very near to speeding it
up too much, or, rather, to provoking an emotional reaction
that would smother the idea under a red tide of wrath. The
man who did most to avert that tragedy was Dwight D.
Eisenhower, who refused to react emotionally to Castro's
opening volley of insults; and it is by no means inconceivable
that future generations may regard this as a greater service
to the country than the command of the Normandy landings.

Even as late as the summer of 1963 the danger was not
entirely eliminated, but it had certainly receded. By that
time the voices still demanding the obliteration of Castro by
fire and steel were pretty well confined to obvious crackpots,
whose influence was dwindling. In the absence of some act
by the Cuban too lunatic for a rational mind to imagine, it
seemed likely that the United States would handle this affair
pretty sanely.

Historically, of course, Castro never was more than a triviality. Santa Anna, the Mexican, was a far more serious threat. Castro's real significance he owed to the general belief of Americans that he was a cat's-paw of the Russians— say, rather, a goad with which the Russians hoped to prod us into blind and ungovernable fury. As far as the game of power politics was concerned, his was a nuisance value, no more.

It is highly probable, however, that he produced an effect that neither he nor the Russians had counted on. He was the means of introducing millions of Americans into a new order of experience, the experience of Alice when she went through the looking-glass and all the world became a mirror image of itself. Our firm conviction that the mirror is a distorting one is irrelevant; it is held before our eyes, regardless of our wishes.

This is displeasing, but that it is permanently injurious is open to doubt. If the republic is a process, it necessarily incorporates all experience, and the value or harm of each experience depends, not on the thing itself, but on the way in which it is absorbed into the plant, or incorporated into the structure. Communism is a fact, an irremovable condition of contemporary life. But its significance to us arises, not from the quality of Communism, but from the quality of our response to it. Dislike, even loathing, is a reaction, but hardly a response. Castro's service is that he has compelled a great many of us to think seriously of what we have said in response to Communism during the nearly fifty years that it has controlled Russia.

Threats are no answer to any argument; but if shaking fists and making faces be ruled out, our reply to Communism really comes down to two expressions, the Marshall Plan and Point Four. Eisenhower's disdainful silence was an effective reply to Castro's taunts, and the sudden appearance of a gun in Kennedy's hand stopped the geographical advance of the Communists. But what effective refutation of their argument, other than the two mentioned, have we produced that wasn't known to Wilson and Harding? If we are candid, the answer is not much.

The fact is, Castro has exposed an abyss before our feet. He has shown us the extent of our failure to persuade the Western Hemisphere, and if our closest neighbors regard our political work as of little worth, what hope is there of our compelling the admiration of Serendip and Cathay? Castro himself is of no importance, but the glare of his lurid career has shown us something that is of very high importance, namely, how close Latin America has come to rejecting with scorn everything we represent except wealth and the power that attaches to it.

Senator McGovern may be right in deploring our obsession with Castro, but something approaching obsession with what has been revealed by the forked lightning over Cuba might be highly salutary. For we have consistently offered our southern neighbors Americanism "as is," not as it ought to be and as we proposed to make it. We have done it because too many of us are ourselves deluded. We have convinced ourselves that this republic is a finished product, not a half-completed structure still covered with scaffolding and standing in the midst of a litter of building material not yet fitted into place. If we admit that there is any work yet to be done, we pretend that it consists of no more than a few finishing touches, not anything essential to the strength of the edifice. Is it any wonder that those of our neighbors to whom our good will is needful turn aside to conceal a smile, while the more independent laugh openly and Castro spits?

Long ago we were, if not obsessed, certainly much concerned with "a decent respect to the opinions of mankind." We asserted publicly that this respect "requires" us to present to the world a clear, unequivocal statement of the reasons for the course we proposed to follow in international relations. The word "requires" is not permissive, it is mandatory, for it unmistakably implies that failure to attempt to make ourselves understood would be indecent.

The Americans who took this attitude in 1776 were aware that they were embarking on an unprecedented experiment in government which the people of other nations could not be expected to understand, without lucid and authoritative explanation. They conceded that the onus of supplying the explanation was upon us, for they were not proffering admission to the comity of civilized nations—we were demanding it; and it is always the business of the applicant to do the explaining. Hence the Declaration of Independence.

But that was a long time ago. The suggestion that other nations still require an explanation of what we are about is incomprehensible to many Americans, for they consider the success of our experiment self-evident. Yet when they are asked to cite the proof they almost invariably begin with our wealth and power. This is to ignore history. In the past the acquisition of immense wealth and enormous physical power has almost always signalized, not the success, but the beginning of the failure of an experiment in government. To prove our success we offer evidence that at best is immaterial, and at worst is testimony suggesting that our failure is inevitable and not far distant.

I believe that better evidence of the success of the American experiment is available, but I am forced to admit that it is not conclusive and sometimes is of doubtful validity. Therefore it should be offered for what it is worth, without any taint of arrogance. By our own proclamation, governments are instituted among men to secure to them their inalienable rights, among which we listed life, liberty, and the pursuit of happiness. Doubtless security and property are both implied, but they are not listed as primary. The phrase seems to have been adapted from John Locke, but he listed "life, liberty, and property," while we excluded property and substituted "pursuit of happiness."

By our own admission, therefore, the relative success of the American experiment is to be measured, not by our acquisition of wealth and power, but by the extent to which American citizens enjoy the inalienable rights with which, we have asserted, all men are endowed by their Creator. To examine honestly and carefully the extent to which we meet this test may be an obsession, but it may be no more than a prudent audit, which unquestionably is desirable from time to time.

Any such test is, of course, highly subjective. That is to say, it is affected by the standards that the examiner applies. My own preference is to use as a base line the average among the other nations that adhere or at least give lip-service to our own ideal of political liberty. It seems to me that from any such test the Republic emerges with what collegians would rate as a B, perhaps even B-plus, but not with an unqualified A. The American, I believe, enjoys a degree of liberty slightly higher than the designated average, but not conspicuously higher, for certain limitations upon his freedom are glaringly evident.

For instance, the American is the only citizen of an advanced capitalist nation who is not free to join the Communist party, if he is so inclined, without incurring legal disabilities, usually pains and penalties. About one third of all Americans are the only members of Western civilization, save Afrikaners and Israelis who are barred by law from marrying where and as they see fit. Americans, unlike Europeans on this side of the Iron Curtain, may be debarred from going about their lawful occasions beyond the national boundaries unless they can satisfy some political jobholder that the journey is in the national interest; the fact that it may be in the American's individual interest is insufficient. Travel abroad by an American against the prohibition of a bureaucrat is punishable by a fine of thousands of dollars and imprisonment for years.

All this is well known to intelligent foreigners, but an astonishing number of otherwise informed Americans are totally ignorant of it, and when it is brought to their attention they are taken aback. Nor can they make a successful riposte when a sardonic foreigner points out that these bonds were not fastened upon them by some conquering Genghis or Attila, but by their own act. They have shackled themselves because they are afraid to be free. Why, then, should they assume the right to instruct anyone in the essentials of political liberty?

There is, as I believe, an answer, but it is not obvious, nor is it available to anyone whose thinking is based on the presupposition that the American republic is a finished product. Such people inevitably come to think of themselves as occupants, not as builders; so when others persist in wielding saw and hammer they are annoyed by the din and, far from praising the work, are inclined to enjoin the workers. Above all, their wrath is stirred by efforts to correct mistakes—to remove a warped or rotten timber and replace it with a sound one. This appears to them an assault preparatory to demolition of the whole structure; and to stop it they are willing to tolerate the enactment of oppressive laws.

If Castro has done anything to jolt us out of that illusion, his existence may not be a total loss. Time may show that he was, in fact, a counterirritant of appreciable value.

On Urban Quasi-Renewal

IN THE SPRING OF 1963 HOUSE WRECKERS, clearing the ground for one of Baltimore's urban renewal projects, reached the alley behind my Bolton Street house, and woe and brickdust spread a pall over the neighborhood.

It was not that we objected to the purpose of the operation. On the contrary, we approved. Urban renewal was a fashionable trend of the times, not at all a local aberration. An American city without an urban renewal program in 1963 would have been accounted a Hickville of appalling backwardness, and perish the thought that the sixth city should have lagged behind, especially when federal money was available.

Nor was this operation a local misapplication of an otherwise good idea. It was quite fitting. Linden Avenue, parallel to Bolton Street one block west, had degenerated. At the turn of the century it had been an upper-middle-class street inhabited, for the most part, by members of the learned professions and by businessmen who were less than tycoons but more than branch managers. It was a street of no great wealth but of very great independence, a street of sturdy characters.

But that was long ago. Invention of the horseless carriage was the beginning of the downfall of Linden Avenue, and it is conventional to lay the whole blame on that contraption,

which is a mistake. Margaret Sanger had as much to do with
it as Henry Ford, taking both Mrs. Sanger and Mr. Ford as
symbols, not as individuals; and there were subsidiary factors
contributing to the result.

The automobile did make it practicable for the owner of
a prosperous but not enormous business to live five, ten, or
fifteen miles from his office. So much for Mr. Ford. Equally
influential, however, was the fact that, unlike his father, he
seldom had eight to fourteen children, requiring a three-
story-and-basement house to get them all under one roof.
So much for Mrs. Sanger. But important contributing factors
were emancipation of the serfs and automation of the
ménage that accompanied it. Emancipation was effected by
the immigration restriction laws, cutting off the supply of
stalwart Polish, Norwegian, and Italian immigrant house-
maids, and of Japanese houseboys; at the same time automation, especially the oil furnace, the vacuum cleaner, and
the electric range and dishwasher, made it possible for the
mistress to take care of a larger and larger part of the house-
work.

In short, all things combined to weaken the holding power
of Linden Avenue and to strengthen the pull of the suburbs.
All of which is a familiar story to sociologists and municipal
politicians from Bangor to San Diego, a story that has been
repeatedly published in every serious magazine in the country. But there is another factor not harped upon with half
as much insistence but which nevertheless played its part,
perhaps as significant a part as any of the others. It is the
fact that the solid burghers who built and inhabited the solid
houses on Linden Avenue did not all go to the suburbs. A
large part of them went into Valhalla, into oblivion, extinction; and I don't mean the cemetery.

The years in which Linden Avenue was built constituted
the era in which the abstraction called "free private enter-

prise" came nearest to realization. The free enterprisers flourished in the interval when corporative enterprise was shifting from the mercantile to the industrial form. The predecessors of the builders of Linden Avenue were the huge mercantile houses that sent the Baltimore clippers into all the seven seas to their branches in Callao, Canton, Madras, and Algiers, and who settled their accounts with bills drawn on George Peabody's branch bank in London. Their successors are the men who today manage the Baltimore branches of immense industrial and commercial networks whose home offices are in New York and Chicago.

The typical Linden Avenue householder was an owner-manager, or at least a partner-manager, catering to the local market; except ship chandlers and shipping agents, who catered to the port. Or, if a professional man, he was a general practitioner of medicine, never one member of a diagnostic clinic; or a lawyer whose face was familiar to all courtroom attendants, perhaps with one partner and forty clients, never with forty partners and one client, after the fashion of modern law firms. Often he was the founder of his business or practice, and always he had built it up. In either case, it was definitely his creation, in which he had a very strong sense of proprietorship.

So, in a measure, was the city in which he lived. He, by his own efforts, perhaps with his own hands, had built some part of Baltimore. Often he had designed and practically always he had watched over the construction of his business premises, and although his house may have been built as one of a group, it faithfully reflected his tastes and needs; so it was his by virtue of more than a title deed. The people made the street, not the street the people; but the street remained after the people had disappeared.

The citizens who fled to the suburbs after the advent of Mr. Ford and Mrs. Sanger were not the burghers. They may have been of the same blood—sons or grandsons of the originals—but they were not of the same type. Linden Avenue was dull, but solid; the suburbs are equally dull, but flimsy. After five years some of them, after ten years many of them, after thirty years practically all of them are ratty-looking. After seventy-five years Linden Avenue was in fact rat-infested, but didn't look it from outside. The population had deteriorated much faster than the houses.

To say that the population that fled to the suburbs has also deteriorated is to take much too cynical a view, but that it has changed is obvious, and that its relation to the city has deteriorated cannot be denied. This refers, of course, to people neither at the top nor at the bottom of the economic scale, but to the middle brackets, greater in numbers than the rich, and superior in intelligence and training to the very poor.

The seventy-five-hundred-dollar man of 1900 stood on an economic level at least equivalent to that of the fifteen-thousand-dollar man of today; but the modern fifteen-thou-sand-dollar men have played no such part in the creation of the modern city and therefore cannot possibly have the same proprietary interest in it. They are neither owner-managers nor partner-managers of Bethlehem Steel, DuPont, General Electric, Westinghouse, Koppers, Martin, Continental Can. They are organization men. Vast numbers of them, five years ago, were in Pittsburgh, Dallas, Youngstown, Omaha, Richmond—anywhere but Baltimore. If they are exceptionally able, five years hence they will be in New York or Chicago, unless they should be sent to London, Paris, Amsterdam, or Rio—anywhere but Baltimore. To them, Baltimore is a waystation, and who has any abiding interest in a waystation?

The flimsy suburbs serve well enough as temporary housing for people passing through. If they are destined to fall to pieces in ten years, what of it? In ten years the organization man expects to be a thousand miles away. Such quarters as were offered by red-brick Linden Avenue were not for him, and the kind of people to whom they were suited no longer exist except in small and dwindling numbers.

The result was inevitable and inexorable decline. The first effort was to subdivide the houses into apartments. It was but indifferently successful, for the buildings were not adapted to subdivision. As better-designed apartments became available, rents declined, maintenance was neglected, less and less desirable tenants moved in. Eventually the street became the line of contact of an advancing Negro and a retreating white population, and that was its finish. The properties by that time had become too squalid for intelligent members of either race; what happened was that the lowest-class whites were the last to get out, and the lowest-class Negroes were the first to move in.

So Linden became an intolerable nuisance, alike to respectable Negroes to the west and to respectable whites to the east. Purse snatchers and footpads, operating from Linden as a base, preyed upon the law-abiding on both sides. No decent woman, white or black, dared venture into the street after dark. A white man was robbed and murdered at the mailbox fifty yards from my house. A white woman was raped and murdered in broad daylight in the next block. The wife of a Johns Hopkins professor was clubbed and her purse snatched as she was putting her car into her own garage four doors from my place. On Linden itself the cops went in pairs, for junkies with switch-blade knives lurked in vestibules and areaways. Stabbed or bullet-riddled corpses, usually of prostitutes, drug addicts, or winos, but sometimes of law-abiding citizens, were removed from the street practically every week. A thriving manufactory of pornographic photographs was raided just around the corner from Bolton

Street. Terrified by prowling rapists and cutthroats, a mother
nailed shut the door to the fire escape from her apartment
and her five children were burned to death. The Health
Department's vermin-control agents confessed utter defeat.

So it had to go. Heaven knows, it never was a Place
Vendôme or Regent's Park, but it had its quality. The
burghers built solidly, and not without grace. Red brick was
their material, trimmed with white marble from the Bare
Hills and Beaverdam quarries just outside the town. Linden
contained no architectural masterpiece, but it had few downright monstrosities, and many of its portals were fine in the
sense that they were eloquent of comfort and hospitality, if
not of the dreams of art. Perhaps originally it was planted
with lindens, but in my time they were planes, nevertheless
good shade trees, and on a brilliant June morning when the
sunlight cut through the leaves to dapple the brick walls,
Linden Avenue was a composition in rose and green and
gold whose light might have baffled Utrillo.

But bulldozers and towering cranes with clamshell buckets
raged through, and Linden rose in clouds of choking dust,
to vanish forever. It had lasted, most of it, fewer years than
I have lived.

This is not intended as a threnody. After silence had followed the din of crashing walls and the first rainstorm had
settled the clouds of dust, Linden Avenue's room was far
better than its company. Its passing is cited merely as visual
evidence of a thing not often seen so clearly, to wit, the
evanescent character of American civilization. From the
engineering standpoint, Linden was good enough to last for
another century or two. Its obsolescence was psychic, not
physical. It could withstand wind and weather, but not
changed social conditions presenting requirements to which
it could not be adapted. So, stoutly built though it was, it
had to go.

But has its going accomplished anything toward solution of the real problem? As regards the adjacent neighborhoods to east and west, yes. Their residents' lives will be appreciably safer and far more tranquil. Present plans are to cover the vacant area with modern housing—high-rise apartments assured of sufficient light and air by being interspersed with park strips and individual houses of one or two stories. Construction will be of steel and reinforced concrete, physically capable of enduring as long as the Tomb of Hadrian, whose walls remain sturdy after eighteen hundred years. We contemplate the blueprints with pride, convinced that they are indications that Baltimore is in the van of civilization. Maybe so—but suppose social conditions change again in less than seventy years? Demolishing the new construction will be a job harder, louder, and dustier than the operation of 1963. This hints at a highly disturbing possibility, namely, that shoring up the social conditions whose collapse doomed Linden Avenue is the real job, to which all the demolition and construction are incidental appendages.

Evidence in support of this uncomfortable theory is supplied by three sources: city people in the areas marked for demolition, city people outside those areas, and suburbanites. But there, in the final analysis, is your city. Certainly it is located on a certain stretch of land. Certainly it includes many structures of many kinds. Certainly a great deal of paving, piping, and wiring is necessary. But all these things are components of a concentration camp or of an army cantonment, neither of which is a city. The indispensable element is people of a certain type, neither prisoners nor soldiers, but citizens.

Among the citizens of Baltimore and no doubt in other cities as well there is a growing uneasiness about the ultimate aim of the urban renewal program. It is generally conceded that the area must not be depopulated. Reconstruction

must furnish housing to as many people as occupied the
area before the program started. This means high-rise apartments, but it does not necessarily mean lack of air and sunlight, if the buildings are intelligently designed and placed.
But it does mean the end of proprietorship. High-rise apartment buildings mean big money, usually public money; for
tax receipts are no more certainly public money than are
the reserve funds of trust and insurance companies.

A tenant has legal rights, but he must conform to all reasonable restrictions of the landlord, so in an important sense
he is there on sufferance, which alters his status not always
to his liking. He is less important to the city, which means
that the city is less important to him. This applies not only
to those persons who are housed in frankly subsidized low-
cost housing, but in any kind of apartment building, including the most expensive although it is perhaps less immediately apparent in co-operatives.

The people who inhabited Linden Avenue are of a different type. Few of them had been resident in Baltimore for
as long as ten years. Many had not lived in any other city.
They were, in fact, displaced persons—coal miners from
West Virginia and Kentucky, driven out by mechanization
of the mines; former sharecroppers, white and black, driven
out by mechanization of the farms. Lacking industrial skills,
they had to take low-wage jobs. Lacking experience of urban
life, they found it hard to adjust. They were in no sense freemen. They were slaves to their own ignorance and super-
stitions. Linden Avenue was not a place of residence, it was
a barracoon, a place of temporary detention of human
chattels until they can be transferred to new ownership.

Of course, urban renewal in Baltimore was linked to a
resettlement program. Other shelter was found before anyone was driven out, much of it in subsidized, low-rent
housing. To some this represented an upward step, perhaps

the first step of a long ascent; but many were incapable of meeting the minimum sanitary requirements enforced by the public officials in charge of the housing; so those tenants who persistently befoul the premises are thrown out and must move on to some other Linden Avenue which in its turn will have to be demolished as a public-health measure.

So what is the real significance of being in the van of civilization? In time to come it may be the bright new buildings; but it may be the coffles loaded with invisible but very real chains, forever shuffling along an endless road, forever just one step ahead of the bulldozers and the sanitary squads.

Then what of the suburbanites, intelligent, educated, trained organization men drawing good salaries, potentially citizens of a fine type? They are spending a year or two or three in Baltimore before being transferred, for better or for worse. They had no part in building Baltimore and expect to have no part in its future beyond a few dozen months. Why should they expend time, thought, and energy upon it? They shouldn't, and they don't. Politically, and to some extent intellectually and culturally, they are an inert mass carried along by the citizens who have stayed put long enough to attain first-class citizenship.

These are the men we are accustomed to think of as the hope of the future, bright, bold, and vigorous. It is measurably true. But they, too, are rootless and mobile. They do not shuffle. They step out briskly. The bulldozers and health inspectors never come near them. But they, too, are under compulsion. They, too, are a coffle, forever moving down a road that has no discernible end.

From the standpoint of the American city, they are hopeless—that is to say, as a type, not as individuals. If they are to realize anything like their full potential, the type must disappear, not necessarily by extinction, but by development of new characteristics that will change it into a different type.

It is just conceivable that this may happen, although it is beyond the capacity of this observer to imagine how. Perhaps as our political maturity increases—assuming that it will increase, not decrease—there may be discovered or invented a new type of citizenship, a type who is not a Baltimorean or a Philadelphian or a San Franciscan, but a city man as distinguished from a country man, with spiritual roots in the city *qua* city and not as any particular municipality. To such a man a transfer would mean only minor adjustments; his civic spirit would be equally strong and equally effective in Louisville or in Detroit or anywhere else.

That is obviously contrary to human nature, but no more so than is most of the rest of what we call civilization. It will require a great deal of study, probably covering a great deal of time; but it would be urban renewal that would really renew and not be confined to an essentially aimless reshuffling of the furniture in the same old room.

 **VI**

On the Inconstancy of the Blushful

IN THE SPRING OF 1963 DR. JOHN ROCK, AN eminent gynecologist and member of the faculty of the Harvard Medical School, created a great stir with a book that, coming from anyone else, would have aroused only scientific interest. It was a dissertation on Dr. Rock's specialty, the reproductive process, and it reiterated what most students of population problems have been saying for years, namely, that a clearer understanding of birth control, widely disseminated, is essential to prevent disaster in the relatively near future. Dr. Rock's acceptance of this conclusion aroused the interest of laymen to an unusual degree because the doctor happens to be a member of the Roman Catholic Church, which is generally supposed to be hostile to the idea.

As a stiff-necked—I indignantly reject the term "bigoted" —Protestant, I have only an academic interest in uproars within the Roman communion. Since in my estimation they are all equally wrong, to me the only noteworthy feature of the affair is not what they say but how they say it; and it is mildly interesting to note that in this controversy, as usual, the holy men put it all over the presumably less holy in the item of venom. Cardinal Cushing, to be sure, spoke of Dr. Rock in lofty rather than pejorative terms, but Monsignor Knott, director of the Family Life Bureau of the National Catholic Welfare Conference, observed that the doctor "has no right to speak as a Catholic"—a decidedly sudden and informal excommunication—and Father Duhamel, S.J., reviewing the book in the Catholic magazine *America*, asserted that the authority on the reproductive process is Pius XII, a dead Pope, not any living doctor of medicine.

This is, of course, nothing new and nothing peculiarly Catholic. The most stiff-necked Protestant must admit that when it comes to haughty and blistering condemnation of an opponent, "new presbyter is but old priest writ large." In political affairs the clerical party is still clerical, no matter whether the particular detachment marches under the banner of Simon Peter or John Calvin—or, for that matter, under the banner of Moses or the Caliph, or even of people not "of the Book." In the efficient generation of murderous hatred Hindu and Moslem have nothing to learn of Catholic and Protestant. The Jew, indeed, claims exemption, but the validity of the claim is somewhat impaired by the historical fact that he has never been in a position to conduct pogroms of his own; and in the art of nourishing hatred for two thousand years perhaps the Jew could instruct them all.

In any event, the theological aspects of birth control are within the jurisdiction of theologians, and it is folly for the unregenerate to pass judgment thereon. Our concern is not with whether Dr. Rock has damned his immortal soul in the world to come; it is confined to the question of whether his theories are consistent with the observed facts in this present world; and it seems to me that they are.

But it also seems to me that the whole matter is, statistically at least, a Christian problem only to a minor extent. The population explosion is of immediate concern to Asia and Africa rather than to Europe and the Americas. There is, of course, the logical possibility that eventually it will become our problem, exactly as the robots, when they started climbing over the wall, became a problem of Capek's humans. But that belongs to the fairly distant future, with which it is impossible for us to deal.

Such is, at least, the impression of a relic of the Edwardian era; yet when I consider the revolution in manners, as distinct from morals, that I have witnessed, and especially the apparent acceleration of the rate of change, I hesitate to affirm that anything is in the distant future. It is logical, I presume, to suppose that anything that can conceivably happen may happen tomorrow. But that way madness lies. To preserve any shreds of sanity, I must assume that some things will last through my time.

I claim the distinction of being the first witness, qualified as an expert, permitted to testify in an American court on a question of obscenity. It was in the Thirties, when a Baltimore bookseller imported for a customer a copy of an English translation of Longus' "Daphnis and Chloë," a pastoral in which the amorous episodes are treated so delicately that today it is regarded as rather prudish. Nevertheless, an inspector at the Baltimore customhouse impounded the book and the bookseller brought suit for its release. The case came up in the United States Customs Court and was heard without jury by the late Judge George Stewart Brown, an excellent jurist, but with his own ideas of procedure.

Plaintiff's counsel was Huntington Cairns, then just beginning to acquire the reputation as scholar and critic that was to carry him to the secretaryship of the National Art Gallery and to the authorship of half a dozen authoritative tomes on philosophy and esthetics. Cairns called a young English instructor from St. John's College and a newspaper book reviewer (me), whom he offered as expert witnesses for his side. As it happened, I took the stand first, which gives me my claim to precedence.

Cairns opened with a series of questions as to the news-

papers and magazines for which I had done reviewing, but
government counsel interrupted.

"Oh, we'll stipulate that the witness is qualified. Go ahead
and ask your questions," he said.

"Have you read 'Daphnis and Chloë?' "

"Yes."

"In your opinion, is it obscene?"

"Object!" said government counsel, and was directed by
the court to explain his objection, which he did for an hour
and a half, after which Cairns took another hour and a half
to point out wherein the argument was all wrong, and, it
then being noon, court recessed until one-thirty for lunch.

As soon as the afternoon session was opened Judge Brown
reached into his desk and produced a ruling on the point. It
covered sixteen typewritten pages, and don't tell me he had
written all that during the lunch recess. Quoting at length
authorities all the way from Milton to Cobb, J., of the
Georgia Supreme Court, he held that while precedent denied
the existence of *expertise* on the point of obscenity, which
must be left to the jury without guidance, there was no jury
present in this case, and the court felt that it had a right
to seek information wherever it might be found; so, he con-
cluded, "the witness will resume the stand and answer the
question."

So at 3:15 P.M. Cairns repeated, "In your opinion is this
book obscene?"

"No."

"That's all."

The English instructor then took the stand and made the
same answer. The judge decided with us and, as the government did not appeal, I believe this stood as the leading case
until some years later when James Joyce's *Ulysses* was
brought into court in New York, and the judge there affirmed
Brown, Cobb, and John Milton, striking off that set of gyves
from the wrists of American fictioneers.

A bit less than thirty years later I was asked to testify in a Maryland case involving Henry Miller's *Tropic of Cancer* but, owing to various legal complications, I was never called. Lawyers move in a mysterious way their wonders to perform, so I have no assurance of what might have happened; but I do not think that on the stand I would have been asked, "Is the book obscene?" I imagine that the question would have been to this effect: "Regardless of whether or not it contains obscenities, is the work pornographic?" My answer would have been, "No," for I understand pornography to mean filth for filth's sake, and Miller certainly had another object in mind.

But the difference in the questions I believe to be a fair measure of the distance that public opinion has moved in less than one generation. It has been propelled by realization that the ingenuity of man has not yet been equal to the task of finding a definition of obscenity that does not fall into one of two inadequacies—either it is a mere list of prohibited vocables, which is to say, mechanistic and dead, or it will include some of the most remarkable products of the human mind—Canticles, for instance, and Hosea, much of Shakespeare, more of Aristophanes, and Rabelais almost *in toto*.

The imbecility of the first kind of definition was luridly demonstrated when John Cleland, a fifth-rate eighteenth-century scribbler, made a bet that he could write the dirtiest book in the English language without using a single forbidden word, and won his wager with *Memoirs of a Woman of Pleasure*, familiarly known—and it has been familiar to college boys for two hundred years—as *Fanny Hill*.

The fatuity of the second kind was as appallingly demonstrated by Dr. Thomas Bowdler, the ingenious nineteenth-century medico who made Shakespeare look like an ass and tried to do as much for Gibbon. The *hubris* of the Victorians, the immoderate pride that made them ridiculous, was typified by Bowdler in their literate strata, and in the illiterate by the vestals who put pantalettes on piano legs. Each was an assertion by the Victorian age that it was purer than any of its predecessors, which, of course, laid it open to the lash of scorn.

This monumental immodesty was due, it may be plausibly argued, to the fundamental error of placing obscenity in the field of morals. It was an error characteristic of the Victorians, or at least the late Victorians, who tended to place everything in the field of morals, presumably because of their crass neglect of the field of esthetics, in which obscenity rightfully belongs.

However, if this estimate is correct, all the current argument over the moral progress or regress of the modern generation, in so far as it is based on the unblushing discussion of once blushful topics, means exactly nothing. *De gustibus . . .* and besides, in matters of taste the movement is neither up nor down but cyclic, or perhaps one should say helicoid, with curves, countercurves, and returns almost, but never quite, to the first position. It seems to me, therefore, that the elated and the horror-struck are equally off the beam, for the alteration that has taken place in my time is semantic, not moral.

John Milton lived three hundred years ago, but when he intimated that "to sport with Amaryllis in the shade" was then a more popular and perhaps a better way of spending one's time than writing poetry, he referred to what D. H. Lawrence described precisely as the pastime of Lady Chatterley and the gamekeeper. The essential difference is not one of morals, but merely that Lawrence, like Pooh-Bah, chose to add "corroborative detail, intended to give artistic verismilitude to a bald and unconvincing narrative." It was an error of judgment in Pooh-Bah, and it may have been in Lawrence, which remains to be demonstrated. But that it is an indication either of an increase or of a decrease in public morality is highly doubtful.

The horror-struck, of course, will be not in the least soothed by this consideration. They cling to the curious delusion that mentioning a fact makes it somehow more factual, hence they attribute moral significance to the mere utterance. Yet piety commits them to the proposition that the two categories into which statements fall are the pleasant and the unpleasant, not the moral and the immoral. "And Adam knew Eve, his wife, and she conceived and bare Cain" is Scripture, "appointed to be read in churches," which is to say, it is irreproachable. Yet a street orator could make the identical statement in terms that would assure his arrest and conviction on the charge of outraging public decency.

As a professional dealer in words I favor, in principle, swift and accurate communication, which implies the utmost attainable lucidity of utterance. But that doesn't settle the matter, for as a trafficker in the parts of speech I have acquired an immense admiration of the beauty of English, particularly the written language. Its syntax, when handled by a master, produces rhythms, cadences, sinuosities, and metrical structures that combine into a music that I believe to be unsurpassed by any other medium of communication. Obviously, a man who can produce the esthetic effects of which English is capable must be one of high intelligence, whose writing will never be empty; but the sound is a powerful reinforcement of the effect of the thought.

Naturally, this convicts me, in the eyes of the symbolists, of being a primitive. I grant it cheerfully, and double the outrage by confessing a decided taste for some whom they scorn as the "tinkling" poets. I read Eliot with pleasure and profit, and I have some respect for Pound for the power in his brutality; but his cacophony I resent because I have yet to find an idea in his poems that could not have been presented more effectively without his arrogant and insulting assault upon the ear. But I would readily swap both Eliot and Pound for

> an old, half-witted sheep
> That bleats articulate monotony,

if the sheep were able to produce one sonnet equal to "Milton, thou shouldst be living at this hour."

The point is that the obscenity of Henry Miller fills me with a distaste that that of "Venus and Adonis" does not, and the difference, as far as I can tell, is that Shakespeare's lines are graceful and Miller's gawky. But what moral significance is in that?

On the other hand, I find tremendous moral significance in the long and arduous but eventually successful fight of Thomas Parran, Surgeon General of the United States Public Health Service, to persuade respectable newspapers to print the words "syphilis" and "gonorrhea" in their columns. Devotion to one's duty is close to a summation of all fine moral qualities, and it is the duty of a doctor of medicine to induce his patient—at least one for whom there is hope of cure—to face the reality of his condition. The Surgeon General's patient is the nation, and Parran compelled Americans to face one of the ugliest facts of their national life, the concealment, which meant the ineffective treatment, of venereal disease.

But that was science, in which there can be nothing obscene because there is no responsibility for the esthetic. Mathematicians, indeed, insist that there is a very high esthetic quality in a perfect mathematical proof; being mathematically illiterate, I must take their word for it; and it was, of course, a very great esthete who reached the conclusion that "beauty is truth, truth beauty." Generally speaking, though, the scientist chooses his word for precision, not proportion. It transmits his meaning; therefore it is inoffensive, no matter how ill-favored.

The literary artist and, on his lower level of endeavor, the literary craftsman enjoy no such exemption. The scientist is permitted to approach truth along the straight and narrow path of the exact; but the humanist meanders toward it across the field of the persuasive. The scientist, seeking to produce his effect in the realm of the tangible, has only to be right; but the humanist, dealing with the intangible and especially with the emotional, is not absolved of responsibility by being right; he must also *seem* to be right, or he will be ineffective. Hence he must have an eye to the esthetic as well as to the precise; and this division of his loyalty is the inexhaustible fountain of his grief.

Thus the fact that a doctor of medicine specializing in gynecology advocates birth control although he is a Catholic may agitate churchmen, but not others. To outsiders, moral significance could enter the case only through a suggestion that the doctor had falsified the evidence, and no such suspicion exists. Then, since a scientist is ineligible to pose as *arbiter elegantiae*, no esthetic malfeasance—perhaps, since a doctor is involved, the term should be esthetic malpractice—can be involved. Which is to say, the event has no general significance, and is scientifically significant only as it happens to be true or false.

But when poets, novelists, and playwrights treat fornication as a parlor topic the situation is different. The esthetic criterion instantly assumes a central position, and judgment hinges not on what they do but how they do it. It was not a cynicism when Burke remarked of the *ancien régime* in France that then "vice itself lost half its evil by losing all its grossness." It was simple acknowledgment that in the artist's creed—and Edmund Burke was a literary artist—ugliness is evil. There is a degree of confusion in that, neatly balanced by the confusion that leads the theologian to believe that whatever he deems evil is ugly.

All of which would be beside the point if it were offered

as criticism of contemporary morals, or even of manners. Clemenceau remarked of the then President of the French Republic, "the two most useless things in the world are the vermiform appendix and Poincaré." Third in order, surely, must be the judgment of a man over seventy on the morals and manners of the rising generation. In the social organism septuagenarians may be regarded to some extent as vestigial remainders; and yet . . .

I have lived from the days when "Daphnis and Chloë" shocked the censors to the day when it took *Tropic of Cancer* to shock them. Length of days has given me appreciation of the irony in the comment of a modern young miss whose taxi was in collision with a truck, and the hacker and the truck driver proceeded to express their low esteem of each other in loud and uninhibited language.

"You know," said the young miss, describing the incident later, "I didn't know anybody ever *said* those words. I thought you only found them in books."

But for me the irony tinges not only the contemporary scene but my guess as to the future. Since I have witnessed in half a lifetime a progression from Longus to Henry Miller, what may one reasonably expect of the American literature that my grandsons, now schoolboys, will read between the ages of thirty-five and seventy?

The mere inquiry throws the pessimist into a state of shock. Extrapolating in the same direction, what could be as far beyond Henry Miller as Miller is beyond Longus? At the question imagination boggles.

But acceptance of the cyclic or helical theory of morals and manners creates a more tolerable state of mind. My guess, offered strictly as a guess, is that American literature a generation hence may parallel my grandfather's standards of taste much more closely than contemporary writing does. I do not predict a return to Puritanism or, to be exact, to

Bowdlerism or an equivalent asininity; but I do predict an increased preoccupation with those structural elements of the language that tend to enchant rather than those that tend to jolt. This may represent a process of intellectual softening, but I do not think so. I find nothing soft in the story of Paolo and Francesca, or in that of Hester Prynne and Dimmesdale; on the contrary, I feel in them a strength not discernible in the account of Lady Chatterley; yet they do enchant.

What, then, of morals? For my part, I do not perceive any progression in any direction in morals that is analogous to the curving line of esthetics. Discounting as utterly un-predictable what new factors medical science may introduce into the equation, I suppose that the biological urge will retain its urgency for the next generation or two, and the prevalence of bastardy will remain approximately what it was when Erasmus and William the Conqueror were born into that ambiguous estate.

The central fact, in any event, is that American civilization is not more than, probably much less than, half finished. It is covered with scaffolding through which we may descry only with difficulty even the main outlines of the finished structure; so why pronounce judgment now?

On Education and the Contrary

IN THE SPRING OF 1963 THE JUNIOR SENATOR from Arkansas, the Hon. J. William Fulbright, and the senior Senator from Pennsylvania, the Hon. Joseph S. Clark, were quoted at length in an "occasional paper"—i.e., a pamphlet —issued by the Center for the Study of Democratic Institutions. The occasion was a discussion staged by the Center on the subject "The Élite and the Electorate," in which the participants were the two Senators, a few guests specially invited to sit in, and two distinguished foreigners, Pierre Mendès-France, former premier of France, and Quintin McGarel Hogg, Viscount Hailsham, Conservative leader of the House of Lords.

The pamphlet received more than usual attention from the press because it contained two statements that, as coming from American politicians, astonished many people.

Senator Fulbright opened his remarks with the dictum, "Government by the people is possible, but highly improbable."

Senator Clark in the course of his remarks declared that "the legislatures of America, local, state, and national, are presently the greatest menace to the successful operation of the democratic process."

Both Senators asserted that the avenue to desirable change is through education; but Adolph W. Schmidt, a Pittsburgh banker who had been invited to sit in, asked how to draw the important distinction between liberal education and technological training.

I believe that both politicians were speaking unpopular truth, hence the general astonishment; and I believe that the banker's point is an important one. But I also believe that my first duty is to acknowledge, to others and especially to myself, that I am construing all three statements in the light of my own experience; so the next man may construe them differently, yet with the same chance of being right.

For instance, Senator Fulbright's statement that government by the people is possible, but highly improbable, obviously involves a misuse, so common that it may be called customary, of the word "government." To be exact, the Senator should have said "administration" by the people, but in that case he would have admitted no qualification. He would have said that it is impossible, and said no more. To ask whether administration by the people is possible is equivalent to asking whether the umpire can play a baseball game. The umpire can govern the game, in the sense of determining its outcome, but eighteen men are required to play it.

The American people can send a lame-brained or contumacious public servant to the showers, but they cannot take his place, any more than the umpire can himself replace a batter who swings on the catcher instead of on the ball, or a pitcher who repeatedly tries to split the batter's skull instead of the plate. In that sense, but in that sense only, the people can govern.

By the same token, Senator Clark's assertion that legislatures—in the same paragraph he explains that he means all kinds, city councils, state legislatures, and Congress—are presently the greatest menace to the successful operation of the democratic process is sustained by the evidence, but in introducing the evidence he should have made one highly important stipulation, namely, that legislatures are in fact as well as in law representative of the people. This lays the foundation for the deduction that they may be obstacles, not because they are legislatures, but because they are people.

Let us here take time out to dispose of the foreigners. M. Mendès-France and Lord Hailsham spoke in broad, general terms, which was to be expected, seeing that the word "élite" is already defined for them. They were heard attentively, but their utterances were not subjected to the critical analysis applied to the Americans because they were not controversial. As a matter of fact, even in the case of the Americans it was the comment of the banker that really opened the way to disputation.

Since the facts adduced by both Senators are hardly open to debate, it is natural that they should have agreed that liberal education widely dispersed is the solution. But the banker wanted to know what is liberal education; and that tripped the alarm. I have no knowledge of his studies, but perhaps he had read Plato. Perhaps he had read John Dewey. Perhaps he had read every important philosopher between the two. If so, he got an answer to his question every time; but if in the multiplicity of answers he could find one that is complete and conclusive, he might set up as a philosopher in his own right, for nobody else has done it.

Liberal education seems to be as incapable of definition as correct esthetic taste, and for the same reason—what it is depends in part upon the student, in part upon his way of studying, and in part upon his motive in seeking education. If you fancy pedantic speech, say it is ontological, epistemological, and teleological, which should be enough to get the dust brushed off any ordinary man's dictionary.

Make it political education, though, and the field is greatly narrowed. Make it American political education and it is narrowed still more, perhaps reduced to dimensions capable of being surveyed by intellects less wide-ranging than Einstein's. The variant *americanus* of the species *sapiens* of the genus *Homo* is a relatively small object, statistically somewhat less than one fifteenth of the population of the earth. He may be small enough for his characters, properties, and attributes to be ranged and ordered with some measure of success.

The only rational aim of political education anywhere is the establishment of order that can be maintained with minimum expenditure of energy, blood, and cash. Americans are committed to the theory that this means order based on justice rather than on force. For us, then, political education means the process of learning to establish and maintain order in that particular form.

My individual preference is to approach the subject by analogy. The proper education of an umpire is directed toward the development of three capacities—sharp sight, instant decision, and resolution enough to make the decision stick. Resolute, of course, doesn't mean bullheaded. A good umpire is not to be intimidated, not even by the bleachers spilling onto the field, roaring; yet if they pull the rule book on him, he has humility enough to reverse a wrong decision gracefully.

It sticks to my mind that a liberal political education is one that will develop analogous qualities in a voter. Without actually participating in the political game by doing any running himself, he watches it narrowly. He cannot be caught napping by a quick throw, nor fooled either by acrobatics or by clouds of dust; and the pandemonium of the cheering section affects him less than the droning of a mosquito would.

This is the ideal voter, like any other ideal only to be approximated in real life; but the closer the approximation,

the nearer we shall come to Senator Clark's "successful operation of the democratic process." It is not perfectionism, it is
merely optimism to believe that we can make the approximation a good deal closer than it is at present; which gives
point to study of the process.

To begin with, it is essential to recognize the division of
education into its two classes, the relatively slight doctrinal
and the immensely larger empirical, or what you learn in
school and out.

For one, I am inclined to think that the proper function
of the college, the higher institution, is not education at all,
but de-education. It is, however, an inclination due to no
logical process, but to individual experience. When I entered
college at the age of seventeen I knew everything. When I
emerged, just short of twenty-one, I had begun to doubt that
I knew anything; and the subsequent fifty years have been
one long confirmation of the doubt.

Yet to be disburdened of the crushing load of misinformation under which I staggered when I entered was a favor for
which I owe my *Alma Mater* a debt that can only be
acknowledged, never paid. It was not that Wake Forest, in
the first decade of the century, was an exceptionally good
college. Measured by its own standards, as of 1963, it was
very bad. Its endowment was minuscule—trustees as pur-
blind as patriotic had sunk its original funds in bonds of the
Confederate States of America. Its plant and equipment were
scanty and for the most part antiquated. Its ratio of instruc-
tors to students was rather above twenty to one. Its faculty
salaries were a scandal. Its students were in overwhelming
majority products of the North Carolina public schools of
fifty years ago, which is to say, miserably prepared. It was
constantly harassed by guerrilla warfare waged by bands
of Holy Willies from backwoods churches who demanded
that the college cram down the students' gullets, with ram-

rods if necessary, a granitic conviction that Jonah swallowed the whale.

Notwithstanding all this, light streamed from its windows over a darkling land. After more than half a century I well remember the first blinding flash that left me with spots before the eyes. William Louis Poteat, opening his course—an introduction to general biology—remarked, "The first thing to remember, gentlemen, is that until you have learned the facts you have no right to an opinion." Never before had that elemental been mentioned to me by any teacher; so right there my de-education began.

It proceeded under John Bethune Carlyle, classicist, who in a Presidential year taught Cicero's "Letters," not out of the book, but out of the Charlotte *Observer*, a morning newspaper. Comparing, day by day, the text with the news stories, he drew parallels, obvious once they were pointed out, between Cicero's advice to his son-in-law, running for some office in Rome, and the maneuvers of the campaigners then raging across the country. I learned little or no Latin in that class, but I did learn that as a smooth political operator Marcus Tullius Cicero could have given cards and spades to Franklin D. Roosevelt and licked him four out of seven. I have since had use for that information, but none for any equivalent of "the doctrine of the enclitic *de*."

The process was capped, it may be, by a remark made, but not in class, by Benjamin Sledd, head of the English department, by birth a Virginian, and how! I have sometimes thought that all the Randolphs, Byrds, and Marshalls between Accomac and Lee were, combined, not as Virginian as Dr. Sledd, whose pride of birth had been greatly accentuated by long residence in Tarheelia. But for all that, he was a salty character whose ideas were not derived from his ancestors and who, although a pedagogue, had never learned to suffer fools gladly.

We strolled across the campus after the final period one afternoon late in May, when the magnolia blossoms and the gentlemen were both out in force enjoying the balmy air. A pair of track men, in running shorts and spiked shoes, trotted by, not speeding, merely limbering up. Down by the rough stone wall that enclosed the campus another pair tossed a baseball, languidly. Sheltered by low-swinging magnolia boughs, a group engaged in what looked suspiciously like a poker game. In the shade of a giant oak lay one man who actually had a book; but unfortunately the book, spread open, rested on his chest and he slept blissfully.

"Johnson," said Dr. Sledd suddenly, apropos of nothing, "I don't care if this place never turns out a scholar, if only it can turn out men."

A college advised by perhaps its most austere scholar to put the fabrication of scholars in second place—gunpowder, treason, and plot! I think the process of my de-education reached its climax at that moment. The stunning shock was the idea that education does not consist primarily of book-learning, for Wake Forest, for all its handicaps, did occasionally turn out scholars. Adams, the Shakespearean authority long an ornament of Cornell; Murchison, successor to G. Stanley Hall at Clark; McCutcheon, dean of the graduate school at Tulane and later at Texas, to mention only the first three that come to mind, were pundits at least one hundred proof.

As for men, well, the Kitchin brothers, Will, governor of the state, Claude, Woodrow Wilson's majority leader in the House of Representatives, Thurman, president of the college; then Bailey, United States Senator, Bickett, governor, and, among my own contemporaries, Broughton, governor, the younger Murchison, Assistant Secretary of Commerce, Stallings of the Marines, who left a leg on the battlefield but returned to write *What Price Glory?*, Howard, chaplain in

the First World War and dead "somewhere in France,"
McMillan, the missionary in Shanghai who defied a Japanese
patrol to shoot as he blocked the doorway to a room in which
Chinese nurses were huddled, Green, medical officer com-
manding the general hospital at Pearl Harbor on The Day—
with me, these pass for men, and with such I am confident
that Sledd, long gone where good Virginians go, would be
content.

I am therefore reasonably satisfied with my formal de-
education. What I lost by being restricted to poor equipment
and archaic methods I made up, and probably more than
made up, by close personal contact with men whose dedica-
tion was of a kind completely new to me then, and which I
have seldom encountered since. My respect for the modern
college, on a new campus, heavily endowed, with plant and
equipment costing twenty times the total monetary value of
the old Wake Forest, with three hundred teachers of three
thousand students, is very high. I note with great pride that
it was the first Southern senior college, privately endowed
and therefore exempt from the Supreme Court decision of
1954, voluntarily to open its doors to Negroes on the same
terms as whites; and I note with glee that a staff member
who wrote a novel satirizing religious fanaticism had his
contract renewed in the face of thunderous howls for his
dismissal.

That the new college is admirable, I am happy to maintain
against all comers; but that it is as efficient as the old one
was at decontaminating youth who come to it infested with
innumerable types of false knowledge, I piously hope but
find pretty hard to believe. For in the old college it was not
accomplished by any recognized method of handling what
are now called "learning situations," unless close association
with cultivated men be called a method. A passing remark,

a lifted eyebrow, a frown, a smile—how can the power of these be channeled into any pedagogical method?

So I emerged from Wake Forest with a parchment inscribed, by a margin so narrow that it had to be expressed in decimals, *cum laude*, which parchment had cost my father the sum of five dollars, the then diploma fee, and which was worth just about the price; but I emerged also with a dawning realization of the vast extent of my own ignorance, which was worth a fortune. For at Wake Forest there was first lighted in my mind a glimmer that the passing years have blown up into a glare—the knowledge that although I am a native, white, Protestant, literate American, and although I have studied for many years, to this day I know far less than I need to know about how to be politically a freeman.

The college, I still feel assured, had cracked the links, but a long time passed before I shook off the chain that bound me to the delusion that George Washington had made me free back in the eighteenth century. What a body of death, as St. Paul said, is the superstition that "American" is synonymous with "freeman"! Yielding to none in my reverence for the *Pater Patriae*, yet I know now that what he gave me was not freedom but merely a fair chance to learn how to be free; and that knowledge, I am persuaded, is the indispensable foundation of anything fit to be called a liberal education in politics.

The fact that this knowledge is still scantily diffused is a threat to our national security by comparison with which the ravings of Khrushchev are mere persiflage. In the spring of 1963 the newspapers carried a story from Kansas City, Missouri, stating that the municipal authorities were considering abandoning that year their former custom of hoisting around the War Memorial, later re-dedicated as the Peace Memorial, the flags of the United Nations, or such of them as maintain diplomatic relations with this country. The action was proposed as a police measure, in the interest of maintaining public order, for in other years vandals had torn down some of the flags, and not only were the crackpots threatening riots, but even such organizations as the American Legion and the Veterans of Foreign Wars were protesting the display of foreign flags on the sacred soil of Kansas City.

What abysmal ignorance that reveals! It is not simply ignorance of how to be free, but ignorance of the difference between love and hate. Patriotism is usually defined as an attitude growing out of love of one's country, but these people base it on hatred of other countries, for not otherwise can they justify insulting the symbol of nations with which we are not at war. Love and hate are both powerful emotions, and when emotions are strong enough, to distinguish them requires a capacity for analysis that is always associated with some degree of intelligence. Mark the word—it is "intelligence," not "education." The Daughters of the American Revolution are not illiterate, but their tendency to equate patriotism with hatred has long been notorious.

It is painful to intimate that even a minority of residents of the Hon. Harry S. Truman's native state rate below the intellectual level of the D.A.R., but there are the facts. Some of them did threaten to riot against the display of flags of nations with which the United States is at least technically at peace.

This, though, was not the colossal proof of American ignorance of the art of being free in the year 1963. The colossal proof was our singular choice of a style of celebrating the centennial of Lincoln's Emancipation Proclamation. That style included setting police dogs and turning fire hose on school children exercising the constitutionally guaranteed right of peaceable assembly to petition for the redress of grievances.

Half a century has passed since Booker T. Washington good-humoredly—perhaps too good-humoredly—reminded us of the obvious truth that you can hold another man down in the gutter, but only by staying there with him. Within my lifetime my native region has made downright fabulous progress in building schoolhouses, laboratories, and libraries, in supplying textbooks and raising teachers' salaries. Twenty years ago the state of Mississippi was spending on schools a larger proportion of its total income than either New York or Massachusetts was spending. Notwithstanding which, in the spring of 1963 the South was still in the gutter, sitting on the Negro, albeit more and more shame-faced about being there. The question then arises: Have the thousands of millions been applied to education, or almost entirely to technological training?

As regards the elementary schools, the question is irrelevant. Reading, writing, and arithmetic are essentially technological training, which is to say, development of the adept use of tools. It is to higher education that the question really applies, and I, for one, accept the theory that its principal application is not to any of the institutions that we call schools, but to the empirical education that a man acquires on the street and in field and factory. The faculty in that vast academy consists, not of pedagogues, but of the straw boss, the foreman, the superintendent, the precinct leader, and the parson, with the men of law and medicine playing supporting roles.

That is to say, every American whose position gives him any influence at all over another man is saddled with responsibility for teaching the art of being free. But how shall anyone teach if he doesn't know the subject, even if he understands the duty? Journalists alone among the secular occupations recognize the obligation, since it soothes their vanity to look upon themselves as molders of public opinion;

but when one examines the record, the way in which Southern journalism—including radio and television as well as printed matter—has discharged this function, one is hardly overcome with admiration.

Yet to intimate that the degradation of the South is attributable wholly, or in the larger part, to dereliction of duty on the part of its journalists would be not only unjust but idiotic. In this respect journalism stands above rather than below other types of Southern leadership, the clergy perhaps excepted. Indeed, the craft can point to a handful of representatives whose courage and ability can bear comparison with those of any of the glorified martyrs to freedom of the press.

One of the most curious circumstances in this situation is the startling evidence that the genuine freemen tended to concentrate in the lower rather than the higher ranks of leadership. More foremen than factory managers were realistic; more college professors than college presidents took risks; more curates than bishops were liberal; sockless denizens of Tobacco Road no doubt composed most of the lynching mobs, but slightly above that level, among the poor but not pauperized, wise tolerance seems to have been appreciably more widely prevalent than among millionaires.

Ralph McGill has pointed out that the reaction against the school segregation decision of 1954 was not instantaneous; there was at first a silence of some weeks, after which the clamor was raised, first by politicians, then by business leaders such as formed the White Citizens' Councils. It was distinctly later, and then by unmistakable invitation, that they were joined by the wool-hat boys.

The attitude of the politicians is comprehensible. The decision—or, to be exact, its implications—threatened all the neat arrangements by which they had been keeping political power in their own hands. No one wonders that the hit dog howled. The mystery is why business and professional leaders could not see that a policy of *apartheid* was detrimental to their own interests. The inescapable inference is that they lacked understanding of the nature of liberty; in which respect they were worse educated than their hired hands.

Senators Fulbright and Clark spoke well in proclaiming education as our hope. But *quis custodiet* . . . Banker Schmidt was the one to raise the crucial question: Who is to educate the educators?

 **VIII**

On the Chasm Between
Operatives and Designers

IN THE SPRING OF 1963 A MEMBER OF THE BRITISH
government with the improbable name of Profumo was exposed as having dallied with a complaisant female who was
simultaneously dallying with a Soviet attaché, and a tremendous hubbub ensued. Profumo was the equivalent of our
Secretary of the Army, so it was apparent that the woman
could have been the means of transmitting military secrets
from London to Moscow, provided the Briton was a traitor
and the Russian a spy.

Investigation uncovered no evidence to support that
theory. In itself the scandal seems to have been no worse
than Alexander Hamilton's affair with Mrs. Reynolds, but
it was horribly mishandled. Profumo was no Hamilton with
courage enough to tell the truth to authorized investigators;
instead he lied, both to the Prime Minister and to the House
of Commons. Then when a wretched quack who had been
taken up by high society exposed the lie, the government
turned on him and prosecuted him so furiously that it drove
him to suicide. This, of course, gave its critics some basis
for charging that the government was more intent on punish-
ing the man who had exposed it than the man who had
disgraced it.

Moral considerations aside, the prosecution of Dr. Ward
was a serious tactical blunder. It exposed the existence of a

call-girl racket that involved celebrities of many kinds—
political, financial, and social. It shook faith, not in the personal integrity, but in the judgment of the Prime Minister
himself; and the revelation that Ward had moved in exalted
circles jarred the social structure. It was too high a price to
pay for the punishment of one informer, even if the punishment had not been defeated by the man's suicide.

All told, the Profumo affair was a sensation of the first
magnitude and it was enjoyed—too greatly enjoyed—by certain classes of Americans, including those who had been
miffed in the past by some exhibition of British *hauteur*,
those whose disgust with the Cliveden set dated back many
years, and those who merely agreed with Macaulay that
there is "no spectacle so ridiculous as the British public in
one of its periodical fits of morality."

None of which is judicious, while the last is utterly unjusti-
fied, for there is a spectacle more ridiculous than the one that
Macaulay named. It is the spectacle of the American public
in a similar fit. But it is not wise, even for the miffed or for
the non-admirers of Hitler's friends, to laugh or even to
"cough sadly behind their hands," as Mencken used to say,
over the Profumo affair. It touches us too closely.

The fact is that, from our standpoint, the British at the
moment are both supersensitive and necessary to our designs.
The result is that they are excessively quick to take offense
at a moment when offending them would be an inexcusable
blunder on our part if the giving of offense is by any means
avoidable.

It takes no Socrates to understand why the British are
easily nettled at this time. They have just taken a tremendous
beating and have lost an empire. This is bad enough, in all
conscience, but it is made far worse when shallow minds
make it read: The British are whipped and have lost "the"
empire.

Great Britain has been defeated, but not by her armed enemies; all such she has beaten to earth. She has sunk under the weight of historical trends that she could in no wise control. That is defeat, and it cannot be read as anything else, despite the fact that she crowded hell with her foes before she started the descent to Avernus.

She has also lost an empire, but it was not the only one, it was at least the third that has slipped from her grasp. She had one in France that was finally extinguished when "Calais" was written on Bloody Mary's heart. She had another in North America that was lost when General O'Hara handed the sword of Cornwallis to General Lincoln, Washington having refused to receive it from the hand of an inferior officer. The end of the third was nothing so dramatic; it went slowly, by bits and pieces, but it was definitely ended when the Frenchman, De Gaulle, vetoed the admission of Britain to the European Common Market and got away with it.

If this seems definitive, let's, as Al Smith used to say, look at the record. From the end of the Hundred Years' War, when England was down, to the defeat of the Spanish Armada, when she was up again, was a period of one hundred and thirty-five years. From the surrender of Cornwallis to the proclamation of Victoria as Empress of India, high point of the third empire, was a period of ninety-five years. Surely, then, it is not unreasonable to allow, say, fifty years from the date of De Gaulle's veto before definitely striking Britain off the list of world powers.

In any event, even in her reduced circumstances, she is still capable of putting in the field a formidable military power which we may need suddenly and urgently.

But the British have other assets which we are certain to need every day and which are likely to be more valuable in the immediate future than either her manpower or her weapons. The greatest of these is her long experience in three fields, those of diplomacy, of democracy, and of finance.

This is out of line with the conventional view, which is that British industrial technology and salesmanship are likely to be of more value to us than anything else. It is quite true that for a long time the British craftsman and the British merchant were the best in the world, and there is no conclusive proof that they have lost their special skills. But the skills themselves have diminished somewhat in relative importance. Technology centers today on production rather than on craftsmanship, and merchandising is more a matter of delivery than of persuasion. But production and distribution are both heavily involved with finance, while international trade in any considerable volume presupposes order, which involves diplomacy and, as some of us believe, democracy. If the British, then, can teach us anything of value about finance, diplomacy, and democracy, we should study it assiduously.

As regards finance, there is hardly likely to be any dissent. The men who through generations maintained the pound sterling as the world's standard currency were masters of their art and mystery. The greatest American financiers have always given them respectful attention, and now that the dollar has become a great international medium of exchange, we need their learning more than ever.

More Americans will question the value of British diplomacy, and it is true that its record of late has not been impressive. But the fact remains that it maintained the *Pax Britannica* for ninety-nine years, from 1815 to 1914, which is a massive achievement. The idea that we have nothing to learn from the British does not prevail among men on the higher levels of our State Department.

It is on the point of democracy that the challenge is sharpest. After all, we began experimenting seriously with democracy nearly two generations sooner than the British, for we started in 1776 and Britain did not become really democratic until after the Reform Bills of 1832. If acquisitions of wealth and power are accepted as criteria, our experiment has been markedly more successful than theirs. Who, then, should be the teacher and who the pupil?

The trouble with that argument is the premise. The wisest Americans have never accepted wealth and power as the only, or the most important, criteria of good government; in their estimation the first criterion is liberty, and the second law, both taking priority over wealth and power. Imperial Rome, fallen centuries before Britain rose, is commonly accepted as the world's great teacher of law; but the British began experimenting with liberty under law at least as far back as Runnymede, which is to say, more than two hundred years before Columbus sailed and more than five hundred before the Declaration of American Independence.

Democracy is simply a means to the end of maintaining liberty under law. Americans are committed to the faith that it is the best means available, but there are others. Britain, for instance, supplements political democracy with a rigid social hierarchy; and in view of the long British experience in the struggle for liberty, her system is definitely worthy of our serious consideration.

It is obviously imperfect, as are all systems of government. The Profumo affair exposed defects, some trivial and one grave, in the system; therefore it ought to be studied seriously, which is difficult on account of the aura of eroticism surrounding it. The official involved apparently did not commit treason, but he put himself in a position where it would have been easy to do so, which was inexcusable and ample cause for his dismissal; but his dereliction was not discovered by his superiors, which lifts the offending to a higher level. All these, however, are individual failings, gravely reflecting upon the persons involved, but hardly upon the system.

The blot upon the system is the savagery of the punish-

ment inflicted upon the informer compared to the mildness
of the treatment of the errant official. Ward was driven to
suicide, Profumo merely driven out of office. It was a typical
reaction of a vested interest to criticism by an outsider; which
is a defect that over and over again has proved fatal to
nations, not democracies only, but monarchies, oligarchies,
and aristocracies as well.

In 1963 the mildly cynical but highly perceptive Richard
Rovere proclaimed the existence in this country of what he
called the Establishment, meaning a class with a vested interest in the conduct of public affairs, comparable to the
recognized ruling class in Great Britain. He cited impressive
evidence in support of the theory; and it is, indeed, the sort
of thing that is to be expected when the public business
grows enormous in volume and complicated in nature. In
such a situation development of a competent Civil Service is
indispensable to successful conduct of the nation's business.
But the Establishment is not a Civil Service; it is arrogation
to a restricted group of authority, not on the operational but
on the policy-making level. The transformation of a Civil
Service into an Establishment is unfortunately easy and
almost imperceptible. It is commonly described as the rise
of a bureaucracy, but it is much more—it is also the decay of
democracy.

Prestige, when it is earned, is a source of legitimate power.
When a man has a record of long and honorable service, his
word carries, and ought to carry, much more weight with the
people than the word of an unknown. But inherited prestige
is as pernicious as an inherited title; it may carry an utterly
unfit man into public office. No candid observer doubts that
if a young American happens to bear the name of Adams,
Roosevelt, Taft, Lodge, La Follette, or, recently, Kennedy,
his chance of climbing high on the political ladder is far
greater than if he is named Perkins. The bearer of an illus-

trious name may never be President, but he can hardly escape being a member of Congress, an ambassador, or perhaps Under-Secretary of something or other.

Up to a point, this may not be a bad thing. Exceptional talent in the art of government, as in the arts of music, painting, and sculpture, often does run in families, and to refuse to take advantage of the fact would be folly. But the moment the mutual protective association begins to operate, it becomes pernicious. For it is of the very nature of mutual protective associations to be unable to distinguish between the artisan and the artist. The reason for being of the association is to boost its members because they are members, not because they are competent. If a member distinguishes himself as an administrator it will, if it can—and it frequently can—boost him into a policy-maker, at which he may be a dismal failure.

The classical example in recent years is that of John Foster Dulles, who, as long as he was told what to do, even when his orders were difficult to carry out, did it with an efficiency and dispatch that not only established his renown but enlarged the influence of the United States in the outside world. But when he was raised to the rank of Secretary of State and his job became that of telling others what to do, he gave us eight years of diplomacy so feeble and feckless that the influence of this country sank to a level it had hardly touched since the War of 1812.

All of which comes to a conclusion that is perhaps the most repulsive that can be offered Americans—the conclusion that the Establishment presents a question to which there is no answer. We began our national career with a proclamation that there are self-evident truths, a highly doubtful proposition; but if there are any they must have become self-evident long ago, so there is no point in seeking them. What should interest us, and all that should interest us, is the truth that is

not self-evident but that must be discovered, if not by acci-
dent, then by conscious effort, which is slow and uncertain.
But a great many of us will not have it so; we demand a yes-
or-no answer and are enraged when we are told that few
questions can be answered that way.

The Establishment, for instance—in Great Britain it produced, contemporaneously, Churchill and Profumo. What
kind of an answer is that? It can be only relative, qualified,
contingent. We are driven back to the old, unsatisfactory,
uncomfortable, and, it is to be feared, un-American maxim
that "eternal vigilance is the price of liberty."

There are few things that the typical American regards
with more profound distaste than eternal vigilance, which
means eternal strain. It is much nicer to regard all necessary
truths as self-evident, to regard searchers for new ones and
questioners of old ones as subversive characters who should
be put upon the Attorney General's list and debarred from
such sensitive positions as those of movie actors, school-
teachers, and pastors. It is nicer, but it is also the kind of
thing that led the Athenians to sentence Socrates to death
and inspired the mob in the streets of Jerusalem to howl,
"Release unto us Barabbas!"

It is true enough that the primary responsibility for keeping administrators administering and delegating policy-
making to men of original minds rests upon the President of
the United States. But if the President himself has been
elevated to that office because of his skill at painting barber
poles, whose responsibility is that?

There is no getting around it: the successful operation of
the democratic process, to borrow Senator Clark's phrase,
rests ultimately upon the individual democrat; and if his
mind is preoccupied exclusively with democracy, which is
the means, ignoring liberty, which is the end, he will make
a mess of it. The real scandal in the Profumo case is its indi-

cation that something of this spirit has affected England, so that cradle-to-grave security has displaced the ancient rights of Englishmen in the minds of the lower classes.

If it has it is serious, but no more so than our own recent infection with McCarthyism and, one may hope, of shorter duration. Far more threatening, because far more difficult to remove, is the superstition prevalent here, in England, and in every other democracy, that freedom is a status to be enjoyed, not an art to be learned, and that bondage to an Establishment is essentially different from bondage to a George III.

 **IX**

On Liberalism, Romanticism,

and Realism

IN THE SUMMER OF 1963 THE LEARNED AND occasionally vitriolic Dr. Sidney Hook, reviewing in the Sunday *New York Times* a book called *The Essential Lippmann*, seized the occasion to climb upon the frame of Mr. Walter Lippmann and do thereon a war dance so fearsome that one was astonished to read it in the *Times,* a journal whose columns are usually anything but hospitable to the eristic.

The gravamen of Mr. Lippmann's offending, in the opinion of Dr. Hook, is that he has misread American history in such wise that, although he began as a Socialist and an ardent liberal, eventually he despaired of the democratic theory, consigning it to the limbo of unworkable systems of government. The infuriated Hook apparently regards this as a perfect demonstration of *la trahison des clercs,* although, unlike Benda, he does not object to Lippmann's descent from the Ivory Tower, but to his subsequent conduct on the ground level. We are invited to believe that he is an intellectual who has let down his own side.

It may be true, but here is a mild dissent. To begin with, there is serious doubt that the book represents the essential Lippmann. It consists of extracts from the immense volume of his work, but whether or not these extracts present the essential man is necessarily a matter of opinion, and in the

case of Walter Lippmann opinion is widely divergent. As
acute an observer as the late Charles A. Beard admitted that
the search for the essential Lippmann was too much for him.
Somewhere—in *The Republic*, I think—he cut down an inter-
locutor who began, "Lippmann says . . ." with the sardonic
inquiry, "Which Lippmann? Lippmann at one time or another has been on every side of every question."

It was hyperbole, of course, but not without its grain of
truth. A man who undertakes to comment seriously on current events as they occur, not waiting until passage of a
decade or two has allowed some of the dust to settle, is
bound to contradict himself because he is bound to discover
his own errors. Lippmann, as an honest journalist must, has
assumed the risk and has had occasionally to pay the penalty
most feared by the intellectual, that of making a fool of
himself. By that fear many have been reduced to silence
when they ought to speak, for it is not the word but the
"word spoken in due season" that is superlatively good. In
the critical moment Lippmann would prefer to be ridiculous
rather than worthless, and it is one of his finest qualities.

Yet despite a lingering doubt that the victim he transfixed
was the right one, the point that the furious Hook drove
home is, indeed, a point. The role of the Tired Liberal in the
American drama of the twentieth century has been a fat one.
He has been on the scene practically without intermission,
especially since the signing of the Treaty of Versailles, and he
has had a marked influence on the tone of political discussion.
Therefore he merits consideration by anyone who aspires to
understand the United States; whether or not Lippmann
belongs to it is irrelevant—the type exists and the serious
student of America must take it into account.

These people apparently fall into two categories, the disillusioned and the truly fatigued, although the existence of
the second class is open to some doubt. Disillusionment usually presents the appearance of weariness, so it is question-

able that any liberal ever really exhausted his liberalism. Yet although it may be semantically faulty, "tired" does convey an idea consistent with the observed facts, so it is not seriously misleading.

My own experience as a fairly attentive spectator for the past fifty years leads me to believe that the Tired Liberal was not a liberal in the first place; he only thought he was. He is the reverse of Father John, the priest in Shaw's *Saint Joan*, who thought of himself as a rock-bound conservative and a ruthless exterminator of heretics. This lasted until he stood by and with his own eyes saw Joan burnt; after which he was an equally fanatical opponent of capital punishment.

At least twice within this century we have been offered the spectacle of persons who were thunderous protagonists of liberalism, until they got a man in the White House who was not only a preaching but also a practicing liberal. Then a close-up view of liberalism in operation in practical politics so appalled them that they pulled their cowls over their faces and bolted, some to become Communists, others right-wing Republicans, but in either case fanatical opponents of liberalism.

I maintain, though, that Dr. Hook is in error when he thinks he sees a taint of moral turpitude in this. The boys were not conscious, intentional double-dealers. They were romantics, and it is characteristic of a romantic to run out whenever he is confronted with harsh fact. Dr. Hook has distinguished precedents, it is true; when Wordsworth turned Tory, Robert Browning wrote,

> Just for a handful of silver he left us,
> Just for a riband to stick in his coat,

but in after years Browning admitted that he shouldn't have said that. The retraction is something that durable American liberals should bear in mind.

It is difficult, though, when we are confronted with the

visible, tangible effects of the romantics' defection. The League of Nations was defeated, but not by the "Battalion of Death" in the Senate; they were too few to effect their purpose until they were joined by many who had been strong supporters of Wilson, but who did an about-face at the critical moment. The New Deal was halted in mid-career, in part by the course of world history, but in part by the frenetic opposition of former New Dealers. If the pass is sold, it is sold, and if it is done by honest blundering rather than by wicked treason, nevertheless it is done. Morally, there was a world of difference between the commanders at Pearl Harbor and Benedict Arnold, but the difference did nothing toward raising the Pacific Fleet from the bottom of the harbor. The Tired Liberals cannot be held blameless for the frustrations of the twentieth century, but unless the blame is assessed equitably, the inferences from the event will be erroneous and worthless, leading to endless repetition of the blunders of the past.

This opinion, naturally, cannot be judged without some knowledge of the attitudes and inclinations of its author. Accordingly, I insert here the notation that I had the honor of casting my first vote for Woodrow Wilson and have never since regretted it; and I voted four times for Franklin D. Roosevelt and have never regretted that. Perhaps it was sheer stupidity that kept me from being disillusioned about these leaders, but I think it was due to the fact that I never believed too much in either of them.

Before he ran for President, Roosevelt had been elected Governor of New York in a year when that state was so bitterly anti-Democratic that it turned against its idolized Al Smith, conclusive proof that Roosevelt was a fine politician. Wilson had lasted for ten years as president of a university, conclusive proof that he was a superb politician. I was a newspaperman, and while I can't quite accept Mark

Sullivan's dictum that the only way a newspaperman should look on a politician is down, my trade had imbued me with an ineradicable belief that politics has never yet produced an infallible savior of the World. So when Wilson occasionally reverted to the iron-skulled Presbyterian elder, and Roosevelt to the slippery vote-seeker, I never was taken aback. It was no more than was to be expected.

On the other hand, I realized then—and the years have only confirmed the realization—that no man lacking the courage of Winkelried and a will of reinforced concrete could have accomplished a tithe of what Wilson did at Paris. Nor could any man lacking profound knowledge of and faith in people coupled with an alert and powerful intellect have lifted a prostrate nation to its feet and inspired it to make the most magnificent fight in its history, as Roosevelt did.

They were great men, both very great men, but, God save the mark! no more than men. What do you call a liberal President, gentlemen? Nothing short of Michael, the Archangel? But that isn't liberalism, that is romance.

We men of little faith are, on the whole, of inferior quality, I suppose, but we are seldom disillusioned, having rarely cherished any illusions in the first place. It is this that convinces me that "liberal" is a misnomer for the unperturbed; yet a more accurate designation does not readily come to mind. The conservative, were he determined to be polite, would say "optimist." What he would say if he were unrestrained by manners is here better left unsaid. My own preference is for "realist," although I admit that it is a bit presumptuous in that it implies ability to recognize reality, which is to say truth; and a claim to know truth is close to, if not identical with, that pride by which fell the angels.

Yet change is the law of life, and "all that a man hath will he give for his life." Acceptance of change, accordingly, is inseparably linked to possession of life. As regards acceptance, there is no choice. The choice lies among accepting it blithely, blandly, bitterly, or mutinously; the radical left accepts change blithely, the radical right mutinously. To accept change blithely and to accept it mutinously are attitudes that seem to me about equally distant from reality because both ascribe to the direction of change a certainty that doesn't exist—the left that it will be certainly good, the right that it will be certainly bad.

The realist knows that it may be either, and the essential difference between the bland liberal and the bitter conservative is temperamental rather than logical. The liberal figures the odds as at least eight to five that any innovation will be an improvement; the conservative sees the same odds that it will be deterioration. Cynics, of course, are a different breed of cattle from either; it is their opinion that change is not a law at all, but an illusion—*plus ça change, plus c'est la même chose*—which renders them impermeable to argument.

Yet even in cynicism there is a chemical trace of truth, as there always is in an ancient and widely dispersed philosophy. The attitude of Americans toward their own political history has been changing constantly since the administration of President Washington, which is the most persuasive evidence that it is a living philosophy. But liberal opinion accepts the theory that the more it changes, the more it is the same thing without accepting the cynic's theory that the change is not real. Liberals hold that any additions to the superstructure that rest squarely on the old foundations are only in a superficial sense changes, just as the repeatedly altered superstructure of Chartres Cathedral was a realization of the dream, if not the design, of the men who laid its foundations.

At any rate, realization that the United States government is still under construction, to adopt the mechanical or, still evolving, to adopt the biophysical view, affords a basis for a philosophy of American history measurably more cheerful than the one that Mr. Hook, rightly or wrongly, attributes to Mr. Lippmann. It is not entirely rose-colored; there is the distinct possibility that the courses of masonry now being added to the national structure may be out of plumb, and therefore the certain prelude to disaster. Or, to shift the metaphor, that what appears to be new growth may be a malignant hypertrophy that dooms the whole organism. However, to lay to the line and to excise a cancer are both technical operations, dependent for their success wholly on the skill of the technicians. If I understand his criticism, Mr. Hook is accusing Mr. Lippmann of having lost confidence in the ability of the architects rather than that of the masons; of doubting the quality of the germ plasm rather than suspecting a remediable interference with the metabolism.

If that is the case, a steadfast liberal can only hope that Mr. Hook is in error, because it is a criticism that cannot be refuted. We do not know that self-government by the method of representative democracy—that is, self-government successful enough to maintain liberty under law—is possible for any great length of time. We have been experimenting with it for less than two hundred years, and any form of government must last more than three hundred if it is to be rated as durable beyond the average. How many Americans ever heard of the empire of Trebizond? Yet it survived under the Comneni for two hundred and fifty years in relatively modern times. Palmyra flourished nearly as long as the United States has existed, and Nineveh and Tyre, archetypes of the evanescent ("all our pomp of yesterday / is one with Nineveh and Tyre"), lasted longer, Tyre much longer. By analogy, we are probably no more than halfway, surely no more than two thirds of the way, to the point at which anyone may assert with confidence either that our system is durable or that it is ephemeral.

It is therefore by no means beyond belief that this country

may run through what was once regarded as a cycle of history in the course of a very few years, covering in a decade a progression that took the nations of former times a century or two; but it is imprudent to predict that it will do so. Mr. Ferdinand Lundberg may accept the challenge to describe the next hundred and fifty years,* but a more timorous chronicler will admire, but not attempt to emulate, his daring.

The observer who realizes that the so-called status of an American freeman is not a status at all, but a process, an experiment through which men hope to learn how to be free, will risk no prediction as to the final outcome. His limit is to quote the mythical faller from the top of the Empire State Building who said in passing the fiftieth floor, "All right, so far." Yet if Mr. Lippmann expresses doubt that the people can rule, the most timid is entitled to ask in return, "What do you mean by rule?" If it means to administer the government, then all doubt is cleared up. No, the people can't. They never have and there is no reason to believe that they ever will. But if to rule means to fix and determine the general course that the government is to take, the debate is wide open and any position is defensible.

For it depends upon the people. Their self-confidence, or lack of it, may be an imponderable, but it weights the scales of history. Mommsen, speaking of the time when the Romans of 270 B.C. were considering launching against Carthage their first overseas adventure, used language that may well be borrowed to describe the situation of Americans of A.D. 1963. "It was one of those moments when calculation fails, and when faith in men's own and in their country's destiny alone gives them courage to grasp the hand which beckons them out of the darkness of the future, and to follow it they know not whither."

*In *The Coming World Transformation*, 1963.

On the Changeable Past
and the Immutable Present

IN THE SUMMER OF 1963 DR. C. VANN WOODWARD, a historian well known in Baltimore by reason of long tenure at the Johns Hopkins, but in 1963 operating out of Yale, published in the *New York Times Book Review* an article with the arresting title, "Our Past Isn't What It Used to Be." The argument was that most people take the past to be whatever historians say it was; and what they are saying now varies sharply from what they were saying at the turn of the century.

The idea is not as heretical as it seems to be. It is merely a development or, rather, an application to modern conditions of William A. Dunning's dictum of fifty years ago, that the effective truth in history is not necessarily what happened, but what men believe happened, because it is upon their beliefs that they act. Dr. Woodward's point is that we don't believe in 1963 much of what we believed in 1913 about events in or around 1863; hence the events of 1863 are producing now effects that they did not produce in 1913. The Emancipation Proclamation is the most conspicuous, but not the only example.

The essay interested me for two reasons. The first is perhaps frivolous; some years ago I incurred scornful criticism by remarking that nothing is more changeable than the past; but I did not document the thesis with Dr. Woodward's

care and competence, therefore excited derision. The second
is that I suspect that Dr. Woodward was influenced less by
Dunning than by his own experience in assembling the
material for his celebrated biography of Jim Crow.* The
punch in the book was its revelation that this mythological
character is not a survival of ancient superstition but a relatively recent creation, dating from the Nineties of the last
century.

If this view is correct—and Woodward's documentation
seems to be bombproof—the implications are assuredly interesting and possibly important. For one thing, it throws
an entirely different light on some of the most spectacular
events of 1963, those centering upon the Negro's demands
for what is usually called the attainment of his civil rights.
This new light reveals it as a demand for the recovery of
those rights. This leads to consideration of why and how
they were lost, and the answers to those questions may have
significance for the present and the future.

It is of record that in the year 1875 the Negro enjoyed
practically every one of the legal rights for which he is now
contending. There was no segregation in schools, which
means little, for there were practically no public schools in
the South at that date. But there was no segregation in
hotels, restaurants, railway trains, or places of public assembly. All the Jim Crow legislation is of later date, most of
it between 1890 and 1900. In 1875 the Negro was in full
possession of the ballot and in most Southern states held
the balance of power between the two major parties. Segregation did exist in the most important particular of all, but
it was not legalistic; in residence, the Negro was segregated
in the South, but no law held him there.

He began to lose in 1876, date of withdrawal of the last
elements of the Army of Occupation, but the process was

*C. Vann Woodward, *The Strange Career of Jim Crow*, 1955.

gradual. It took about twenty-five years to reduce him to the state of virtual peonage in which he lived until he began to emerge after the First World War and which he had not entirely shaken off in 1963.

There are various explanations of this regression, and in some of them there is a tincture of truth; but most are so fanciful that by comparison they make the story of Cinderella and the Glass Slipper look as factual as a balance sheet drawn by a C.P.A. The most monstrous, and the simplest, is the one favored by such dreamers as Howard Fast (white) and James Baldwin (Negro). This is the theory that in or about the year 1876 the entire white population of the United States went to hell in a hack, with the spirit of Benedict Arnold dominant in the South and that of Judas Iscariot in the North; it was agreed between the two that the Declaration of Independence and the Constitution should be burned by the common hangman, and with the White House representing the thirty pieces of silver, Arnold would purchase from Iscariot the right to re-establish the Peculiar Institution in everything but name.

The charm of this fantastic nonsense is twofold: in the first place, it lays all the blame on dead men; and in the second place, it is simple and so releases us from the hideous necessity of thinking. No wonder it is widely popular and has become an article of faith with the lame-brained.

Unfortunately, it will not stand the test of practical application as a guide to contemporary action. If it were true, we should have only to revoke the infamy and all would be well; but revoking an infamy that never existed solves no present problems.

The unpalatable truth is that the Negro lost his civil rights because he, himself, convinced the North that he was abusing them. The truth is unpalatable because to shallow minds it seems that to accept it one must accept the racist

theories of such lunatics as De Gobineau, Houston Chamber-
lain, and Adolf Hitler. Even those Americans who hold
Samuel J. Tilden and Rutherford B. Hayes in slight esteem
are unwilling to consign them to the circle of the Inferno
occupied by those three. But we are not in fact driven into
any such corner. It is entirely possible to admit that the
Negro lost his civil rights by abusing them without ascribing
to him a biological and irremovable inferiority. All that is
necessary is to remember that abuse of anything almost
invariably follows from ignorance of its proper use.

In the instant case, however, this involves a considerable
and often painful readjustment of our thinking about the
republic and its historical processes. For one thing, it involves admission that the sacrosanct Fourteenth Amendment,
in the form and at the time of its adoption, was less divinely
inspired than boozily romantic. "No State shall make or
enforce any law which shall abridge the privileges and immunities of citizens of the United States" is the language of
a drunk—confused, contradictory, divorced from reality. A
law is not a law unless it abridges some privileges and immunities of somebody, and the same amendment says that
"all persons" born or naturalized within the United States
are citizens thereof. What the amendment really declares is
that no state shall make a law.

The Supreme Court's application of "the rule of reason"
has avoided the disruption of government that would have
attended literal enforcement of this provision. But the typical
American has not applied the rule of reason to the Court's
application of the rule of reason. That is to say, the layman
refuses to admit that the Court has done what it obviously
did; he chooses, instead, to believe that it has sustained
the language of the provision instead of neatly rendering it
void. The layman does not concede, in fact does not understand, one of the basic principles of our system, namely, that

the judiciary, in interpreting any enactment, is obligated to proceed on the theory that the legislative is not half-witted; thus if the language presented to the Court is idiotic on its face, an interpretation of the language must be found that will not impeach the sanity of the correlative branch.

Adhering to this principle, the Court has held that what the Fourteenth Amendment means is that when privileges and immunities are abridged, they must be abridged *en bloc*, not selectively on a basis of categories—racial, religious, economic, or any other except criminal. In all civilized countries, of course, a criminal forfeits all privileges and immunities and most of his civil rights as well; but this does not have to be spelled out in every enactment.

The cold fact is that the Fourteenth Amendment was a drunken enactment, although the intoxicant was not alcohol; it was the passions released by a fratricidal struggle. But the effect in blurring the judgment and producing a false exaltation is precisely that of an overload of firewater. Yet when a nation, even as a man, sobers up, it finds that what was done is done and there is nothing left but to make the best of it; and a nation is even more reluctant than a man to admit that it was, or ever could be, completely plastered, so its efforts are directed to squirming out of the consequences.

The inclination was reinforced in the case of this amendment by the fact that the end aimed at was reasonable and right. The end was the transformation of the former slaves into freemen; and if the means employed were so defective as to make the end unattainable for a century, the reason was an inadequate comprehension of the difference between a freedman and a freeman. For this the Negro must be held blameless; he had had no opportunity to learn. But white men with a classical education knew it, and their inability to communicate their knowledge was the tragedy of the time.

It is more. Note the tense of the verb—it *is* more because

it still exists, reduced, we may reasonably hope, but not
eliminated. To this day the superstition is widespread that
freedom was like one of the elder Rockefeller's dimes,
that it could be handed out to anyone on whom the donor
chose to bestow it. But that is true only of emancipation,
which is not freedom. Emancipation converts a former slave
into a freedman, but that, as the ancients understood but
we forgot, is a status very different from the process that
is freedom. An outside power, as, for example, the armies
commanded by Ulysses S. Grant, can make a slave a freedman; but only the man himself can make him a freeman.

In 1863 Lincoln could proclaim that every slave should
be a freedman, and Grant's bayonets could and did make the
proclamation good. But neither Lincoln in 1863 nor any
power existing in 1963 could make a single freedman a
freeman. The question is: How many have done it for
themselves? And the question is a great deal more important
as it is applied to white Americans than it is as applied to
black. For only one who is himself relatively a freeman
can understand the effort that it takes to be free, and
therefore can judge accurately the effort, if any, that other
men are making to become free.

Inability to make this judgment was the prime factor
in turning fire hose and police dogs on school children in
Birmingham, Alabama. It is characteristic of the freedman to
be inordinately fearful and jealous of others in his own
class. The great need of Alabama and Mississippi is not
freedom for Negroes, but for white men; for were they really
free they would know that the progress of freedom among
Negroes is the only effective guarantee of their own security.

Yet for Americans living north of the Potomac to curl
the lip at Alabama and Tennessee is to repeat the sin of the
Pharisee. He thanked God that he was not as other men, and
he was quite right; he was worse. The Publican came nearer

being justified. Confronted with a lesser menace, Detroit and Chicago respond with a rage blinder and more murderous than that of Birmingham and Jackson. The white man's attitude is not determined by whether he is a southerner or a northerner, but by whether he is or is not terrified. This does not apply to the minority of genuine freemen, wherever they live. Their influence, fortunately, is very much greater than their numbers, which is the country's hope, for they may be able to restrain the freedmen, white and black, until they gain some comprehension of the nature of liberty.

For it is going to be a near thing, especially for the South, but for the rest of the country too close for comfort. The Negro has developed leadership with a working knowledge of freedom. That was proved on August 28, 1963, when nearly two hundred thousand people, mostly Negroes, met in Washington "to petition for the redress of grievances" with only two arrests for disorderly conduct, neither of them a demonstrator.

But there are nearly twenty million Negroes, half of them concentrated in the southeastern states. They are going to acquire their legal rights, certainly the right of the ballot. We may as well face the fact that this means weighting the electorate with a ponderous mass of ignorance and political immaturity, and half of the weight will fall upon a section in which ignorance and political immaturity are already greater than the national average.

The South is in for an ordeal that will strain the fabric of the democratic structure to the limit for a good many years, barring the intervention of a miracle. Nor will the rest of the country escape unscathed. It is highly probable that a politically immature electorate will be victimized by demagogues of a type that will make the Bilbo-Eastland-Joe McCarthy type look like statesmen; and the damage they will inflict when they arrive in Washington will not be restricted to the states that sent them. For the ten years or so after the Negro gains his full legal rights the political atmosphere around the Capitol is likely to be murkier, not clearer, than it is now.

It is nevertheless something that has to be faced. We should have gone through this between 1865 and 1885, but we didn't. North and South alike were so thoroughly poisoned by the hatreds engendered by war that rational statecraft was not humanly possible. Perhaps instead of lamenting that the Fourteenth Amendment was so badly drafted, we should be filled with wonder and awe that it was no worse.

Be that as it may, the trend of events since that time has followed a familiar course. Confronted with what seemed to be a hopeless situation, we resorted to ducking, dodging, and evading with an agility and ingenuity that sustained the farce for nearly a hundred years; with the exception of a few wise and farsighted men who worked steadily, and for the most part obscurely, laying the foundations for a more solid political and social structure. Many of them were white southerners, others white northerners, and it is in no small part due to them that the Negroes were able to develop the leadership that managed the extraordinary display of political maturity in Washington.

But that leadership, whether white or black, is now approaching its most rigorous test, which will come after the Negro is in possession of his full civil rights to the extent that the law can guarantee any rights. The task is to prevent another fiasco comparable to that of 1876. The evidence that they will succeed is of a kind that would not be admitted in any court of law. On the face of the facts, the great mass of the Negroes, having all their lives been excluded from any effective participation in self-government, are unprepared to assume the responsibilities of citizenship in a democracy. But this ignores a fact that history has proved a hundred times over—the fact that under fearful tension people learn fast. The American Negro has been under increasing tension since the First World War, and in the past five years the tension has become fearful. They are not the same people that they were even one decade earlier.

By the same token, the white South, too, has been learning with a rapidity little suspected by the rest of the nation. Doubtless it would have been wiser to have learned in an easier way, but that is water under the bridge. All that counts is that it has been learning, and this introduces an element of doubt into the prediction made above, namely, that a rather dreadful period is immediately ahead. If both races have learned fast enough, the immediate future could be the very reverse of that prediction.

The prudent forecast is for a period difficult enough to subject the patience of the whole American people to a severe test. But what of it? What are we here for, if not to learn by trial and error the utmost of which the political method of representative democracy is capable? If it breaks under the strain, then the rest of the world will know just how far it can be carried; but if it doesn't break, we are committed to carry it further.

"In order to form a more perfect Union, establish justice, insure domestic tranquility, provide for the common defense, promote the general welfare, and secure the blessings of liberty to ourselves and our posterity," we, the people, established and ordained the Constitution. Can any rational man delude himself that this work has been completed? Does not candor compel the admission that it is hardly half done?

When I was a small boy I thought that George Washington had made me free once for all. The small Negro boys with whom I played thought the same way, except that they substituted Abraham Lincoln for Washington. I wish I could add the words of St. Paul, "But when I became a man, I put away childish things." I would except for the question: Have I ever become a man? Physically, yes. Emotionally, in part. Intellectually, perhaps. But politically? That is the question to which only the future can supply a conclusive answer.

All I am sure of is that Dr. Woodward is right. Our past isn't what it used to be. When I was a child, the past was over and done with; but now "the past is prologue."

 **XI**

On the Indispensability of Ogres

IN THE SUMMER OF 1963 THE PRESIDENT OF THE
United States—the Prime Minister of Great Britain con-
curring—offered for ratification by the Senate a treaty with
Russia so bad that, as Churchill said of democracy, all that
could be said in its favor was that everything else suggested
was worse.

The treaty was an agreement among the three signatories
to set off no more nuclear explosions in the air, under water,
or in outer space, the agreement to stand until ninety days
after its denunciation by one of the contracting parties.

It was not much of a treaty. It left the three nations free
to conduct as many underground tests as they liked, to
construct as many launching pads as they liked, to fabricate
and store as many atomic warheads as they liked. The only
dangers it eradicated, or at least reduced, were both hypo-
thetical—the danger of poisoning the atmosphere with radio-
active fallout, and the danger of interfering with radio communication by disrupting the ionosphere with explosions in
space.

Nevertheless, it was a treaty, the first negotiated with the
Soviets in the field of atomic weapons; and it was received
with an outburst of denunciation of extraordinary virulence.
It is incredible that a pact as innocuous as this one could
have aroused such passion in and of itself, and in fact little

effort was made by its opponents to attack its provisions.
It was assailed, not for what it contained, but for what it
symbolized. It was regarded as the initial number of a series.
The senior Senator from Georgia, the Hon. Richard B. Russell, told a convention of the Veterans of Foreign Wars,
"After one ratification in this area succeeding ones become
easier through rationalization such as 'we can't stop now.' "

The Senator did not bother to explain why that would
be a bad thing. Yet all history shows that serious conflicts
of interest between large nations are seldom, if ever, adjusted
at the first effort. The normal procedure is step by step, first
clearing minor disputes out of the way and not until they
are disposed of even approaching the big problems. The
supporters of the treaty approve it for the very reason that
Senator Russell cited against it.

Other critics shied around this argument, but they advanced another, equally dubious. It was the flat assertion
that if the treaty were ratified the Russians would certainly
cheat, to our serious and perhaps ruinous disadvantage. This
is open to two objections, both deadly. The first is that it is
based on the assumption that the Russians could and would
cheat us more effectively than we could and would cheat
them. This assumption is not sustained by the historical
evidence. The second objection is that the argument assumes
that it would be to the Russians' advantage to destroy the
basis of the law of contract, which presupposes a modicum
of good faith on both sides. If good faith is non-existent,
contract is impossible and all international relations are reduced to a skin game.

That the Russians have frequently broken faith seems to
us evident, although they deny it with heat. But if they
were totally devoid of this quality they would be unique
among the nations, and they are not. At least two years
before this treaty was negotiated I had the pleasure of

lunching in the captain's cabin of a ship lying in Baltimore harbor. The captain told me that he had just discharged a cargo of manganese ore consigned to the Sparrows Point steel mills, which cargo he had loaded at Batum, a Russian port on the Black Sea.

An American corporation, the Bethlehem Steel Company, had contracted with the Russian government, through intermediaries, I suppose, but of its own volition, for the ore, and had incurred the expense of sending a ship to Batum to pick it up. Nobody doubted that the Russians would promptly deliver, which they did. Throughout the Cold War, trade with Russia in non-military commodities has been continuous and often direct. But it would have been impossible in the absence of any measure of good faith. The Russians, as surely as anybody else, will fulfill a contract when it is to their advantage to fulfill it; and they are certainly not the only ones who will try to wriggle out of a contract that proves to be unprofitable.

Unquestionably, the practice of cheating in international relations is widespread. It is also ancient. The cynicism that an ambassador is a man who goes abroad to lie for his country is much older than the U.S.S.R. Furthermore, in the rest of the world the opinion is prevalent that when it comes to stacking the deck Uncle Sam is about as deft an operator as any on earth. If that is a slander, the fact remains that the danger of being swindled cannot be a consequence of this treaty, since the danger antedated the treaty by uncounted centuries. It cannot, therefore, account for the frenetic opposition.

It is the alternative that really terrified a considerable number of Americans. The alternative is that Russia might make good in the matter of abandoning atomic tests. If she did, the foreboding of Senator Russell would be justified —the temptation would be strong to make another deal with her touching some other abrasive point of contact, and that might lead to another. It is hard to believe the issue of Berlin would be soon resolved, but fishing rights might be, and after that possibly Formosa, or even Cuba. Eventually we might get around to Berlin and find ourselves dealing with Russia with little more reserve than we now maintain in dealing with Italy or Spain or Argentina.

To Americans of a certain type this is intolerable, not because they consciously pant for war with Russia, but because it involves demolition of the Ogre, and they would be put to the trouble of discovering or inventing a new one, because they cannot envisage life without an Ogre. The Devil, who played the part beautifully for centuries, is now too dilapidated to be of much use. In the eighteenth century Burns commanded general assent in affirming that

> The fear o' hell's a hangman's whip
> To haud the rogue in order,

but if Carl Sandburg made the same pronouncement today, he would evoke more giggles than applause.

But if not the Devil, then what? For the past century the rogue that Jonathan Edwards could reduce to conformity by dangling him over the mouth of hell has been kept in line by the whip of "foreign isms." Anarchism, Socialism, Bolshevism, and Communism have served, chronologically, in that capacity. But if by a succession of reasonably satisfactory deals Communism should be shorn of its preternatural efficacy, and the idea should spread among the rogues that Commies are not appreciably more damnable than wops, hunkies, sheenies, and spicks, the successors of Jonathan Edwards would be disarmed; and it is their immutable belief that if such a thing should come to pass moral superiority would perish from the earth.

It would not, but trying to convince the morally arrogant

that it would not is as useless as Cromwell's advice to the Scotch Presbyterians that they should pray God to show them that it was possible for them to be mistaken. The morally arrogant can be persuaded only by John Hay's method of convincing a member of the House of Representatives—take a stick and hit him on the snout.

That has been effective from time immemorial, but it is drastic, and in an explosive situation drastic methods are not to be recommended. As for Cromwell's alternative, the bald fact is that we cannot be sure that the morally arrogant are mistaken. The equivalent of a hangman's whip—that is to say, fear in some form—perhaps is necessary to hold the rogues in line. Otherwise they could not be relied on to return to Congress, term after term, some Little Brother of the Rich with no more interest in the welfare of the mass of his constituents than he has in tracing the orbits of the twelve moons of Jupiter. The ejection of such a character from the House would be the reverse of a decline in public morals, but the nobility and gentry do not believe it.

That is to say, it is not the dominant belief among the privileged classes; but it would be a mistake to say that it is not present at all. In this country, at least, Cromwell's advice is sometimes accepted. I know that, not by hearsay, but by experience. Not once only but repeatedly I have seen Americans whose political maturity I had regarded—and on strong evidence, too—as approximately that of Neanderthal man yield their preconceived opinions under no pressure other than that of additional information, and become not merely contemporaries but highly effective leaders of the modern age.

The most conspicuous example that comes to mind is that of the late George W. Norris of Nebraska. It is probably too much for the rising generation to believe, but it is of record that Norris, not only when he first entered public life but afterward until he had climbed to the Congressional level, was as hidebound a partisan as the whole area "from sea to shining sea" could produce.

Even after Norris, by leading the revolt against Czar Cannon, had broken the chains of extreme Republican orthodoxy his thinking remained parochial. He was one of the "Irreconcilables," the Battalion of Death, around which that master of devious politics, the elder Lodge, organized the forces that eventually brought about the defeat of the League of Nations. Norris honestly opposed the whole idea. Lodge, on the contrary, had gone on record as favoring the principle of collective security; what he opposed was letting the Democrats get credit for establishing it. Norris would have despised that as a motive, but he let himself be used to effect it, evidence of political immaturity.

It took the Teapot Dome scandal, followed by the panic of 1929, to awaken him to reality. It may be argued that he was, in a way, subjected to Hay's treatment; but it wasn't a stick with which he was hit, it was Hercules' club, swung by no man, but by the mighty arm of Destiny. The point is, though, that when Norris did mature, he matured completely. His long, lonely, bitter, but eventually successful fight for the Tennessee Valley Authority was as fine an achievement of farsighted statecraft as that era produced; and Norris, once the serf of narrow prejudice, died as completely a freeman as any member of his generation, far more free than most.

Less conspicuously, in measure as he was less powerful intellectually, Vandenberg of Michigan followed a similar course; and even Robert A. Taft, almost as adroit a politician as the original Lodge, in his last years admitted that part of his early opposition to social change had been mistaken, and energetically promoted policies that he had once denounced.

As evidence of national maturity, however, the conversion of any number of politicians is not as significant as the change in tone of American business philosophy—using "philosophy" in this connection simply as a name for a businessman's conception of the meaning of business, how he answers the question: What justifies a rational man in devoting his energies and the best years of his life to this form of activity?

If that question had been put to a significant number, say a thousand, of American business leaders, and if it had been asked twice, first about the time I graduated from college and again today, I think the answers would reveal a significant shift of opinion during the intervening half century.

Even today a considerable proportion of the honest answers would be "money" or its equivalent, as "livelihood," "status," or "success." But I believe, although admittedly without the kind of evidence admissible in a court of law, that the proportion of more complex answers would show a striking increase. Be it remembered that we are questioning not simply businessmen, but business leaders, persons whose intelligence and energy both rate above the average and who rank as policy-makers rather than merely managers. Statistical evidence, admissible even in court, does show an enormous increase during the past fifty years in the noncommercial activities of American corporations, proof of a different kind of thinking on the policy-making level. Corporations are practicing sociology, preventive medicine, general education, and even psychiatry on a great and expanding scale, for which the men at the top must be responsible.

Many foreign observers have noted with astonishment the number of large American business concerns whose practices as regards labor relations are distinctly more socialistic than anything that the socialist governments of Europe have dared try. What did it? Why, the Devil and Daniel Webster (with apologies to Mr. Stephen Benét). It is true that it is difficult to cite a match for Norris or Vandenberg among business tycoons. The relative stability of the power of money, as compared to the power of political skill, deprives the successful businessman of the suppleness of mind essential to the survival of the politician.

But in the course of fifty years the Devil carried them off, if not into the cemetery, then into retirement, making room at the top for men in whom the process of mental ossification has not gone so far. These, retaining something of the Yankee ingenuity traditionally typified by Daniel Webster, are able to understand that a new age demands new ideas. For instance, these men can see that the inventiveness expressed in automation has economic effects that go far beyond the necessity of retooling; thus automation has been a catalyst precipitating an interest in social problems aforetime held in solution in businessmen's minds, if present at all.

This is, at least, the politer explanation. The less polite is simply that the collapse of the economy in 1929 threw the fear of God into them and that it has persisted more or less ever since.

Let that pass. My observation, fairly continuous since the accession of King Edward VII in England, leaves in my mind the impression that among politicians and, more significantly, among businessmen the twentieth century has witnessed an appreciable weakening of faith, once all-powerful, in the hangman's whip as absolutely necessary to hold the rogues in order.

Let it be repeated for emphasis, this refers to able politicians and able businessmen; but any age is entitled to be judged by its best, not its worst, products. We measure Elizabethan England by Shakespeare, not by the semi-literate pamphleteers and woeful poets that swarmed in London in those days. We measure revolutionary America by Washington, not by Horatio Gates. There is then no equal justice in measuring twentieth-century American politics by Albert B. Fall and its business by Billie Sol Estes.

It is not beyond belief that an acidulous reader may at this point interject the query: "And its philosophy? Are you intimating that it should be judged by another twentieth-century product, Pollyanna, the Glad Girl?" Well, not exactly. Pollyanna and Dr. Pangloss were both considerably more confident of the accuracy of their deductions than I am. I know that it is within the bounds of possibility that Gunnar Myrdal's estimate of our "affluent society" may be sounder than Galbraith's, and if the dour Swede does know what he is talking about, the level of puerility in our economic as well as in our political thinking is still dangerously high. Myrdal, emphatically no Pollyanna, envisages the possibility that it may soon run fatally high; and if it does, it will be pretty sure to put a dismal end to the experiment begun in 1776.

But is it in fact rising? For one, I venture to doubt it and see two or three reasons for cherishing the hope that it may be subsiding. For instance, it is certainly arguable that the debates in Congress, always keyed to the general level of intelligence, during the Cold War have been appreciably less imbecile than they were in the comparable period between the Mexican and Civil wars; and I lean to the view that the Cold War debates have showed an accretion of sanity over those of the Long Armistice. True, if criticism grows precisionist, demanding an exact measurement of the difference in rationality between Tom-tom Heflin and Joe McCarthy, the thing becomes the calculus of the infinitesimal, at which I claim no competence.

More to the point is the evidence of a higher degree of realism in the thinking, or at least the talking, of the masses of Americans who are neither Congressmen nor tycoons and do not seriously aspire to be either. The "monkey law" that precipitated the Scopes trial at Dayton, Tennessee, in 1925 still blots the statute books of several states, but there has been no repetition of the trial, and the original one has been made the theme of a moderately satirical play on Broadway. The Bible-in-the-schools decision of the Supreme Court did reveal a disconcerting persistence of the belief in word magic, but sixty years earlier as popular a President as Theodore Roosevelt almost blasted his own political career by ordering what he regarded as the smugly hypocritical motto, "In God We Trust," eliminated from the coinage.

Of course it may be argued that against these modest gains the cult of the indispensable Ogre is a crushing counterweight. But why? The Ogre has always been with us in some form. By the time Jonathan Edwards' God-As-Flame-Thrower began to fade, the Declaration of Independence was erecting dim-witted old George Hanover into an incarnation of all the evils of British parliamentarianism; and after him came a long procession of dragons, usually pasteboard stuffed with sawdust, but sufficiently fearsome of aspect to drive the donkeys into the corral. The omniscient, omnipotent, and omnipresent Communist is only the current representative of a long line of wind-inflated monsters that reaches as far back as we can peer into history; but as a counterweight against our progress in learning how to be free, no one can prove that it is heavier than the earlier ones, and there is much doubt that it is as heavy.

Unquestionably the Communists are bad actors, and if Uncle Sam were fool enough to present his back to them he would probably get a knife in it. But the whole idea of the republic is fantastic unless Americans have at least rudimentary brains, enough to prevent them from deliberately inviting murder. Granting so much, it follows that in measure as they master the art of being free the Ogre becomes dispensable. Naturally, this displeases those whose secret wish is to hold them forever in villein socage, not to say chattel slavery; yet a realist can see evidence for as well as against the theory that we are slowly mastering the art.

 **XII**

On the Prescriptions of Three Doctors

IN THE AUTUMN OF 1963 THE INDUSTRIOUS AND undeniably illustrious Dr. Gunnar Myrdal published a book challenging certain conclusions of the equally industrious and illustrious Dr. J. Kenneth Galbraith, author of *The Affluent Society*, and having overtones weirdly echoing observations of the industrious and illustrious Dr. Milton Eisenhower, author of *The Wine Is Bitter*.

This chain of events could hardly escape the attention of any inquisitive mind, if only on account of the disparate situation of the three scholars. Dr. Eisenhower is a brother of the former President, therefore obviously an Eisenhower Republican, as well as president of the Johns Hopkins University. Dr. Galbraith, sometime of Harvard, later adviser to President Kennedy, and afterward Ambassador to India, is equally obviously a New Frontiersman. Dr. Myrdal, among many other things a professor at the University of Stockholm, is a Swede, so necessarily a practitioner of un-American activities.

The concurrence and, less importantly, the divergence of such oddly assorted types as they consider the state of the nation cannot fail to be instructive and possibly edifying to any American who gives the matter close attention. The books—Dr. Myrdal's title is *Challenge to Affluence*—form a triad, although Galbraith wrote before the others and

Myrdal and Eisenhower almost simultaneously, but apparently without consultation. Yet they converge upon a single point, conclusive evidence that it is a point of high significance.

The point is that the United States, like "the gallant Hood of Texas," who, according to the Confederate infantrymen, "played hell in Tennessee," has made a godawful bust of things since it moved into the unfamiliar territory of social and economic problems. The consensus of the learned doctors, viewing the record from widely different angles, is that the explanation may be what is implied by inserting "and" between "social" and "economic." The problem, they agree, is basically one—the socio-economic problem, "now and forever one and inseparable."

True, beyond that point they diverge. Dr. Eisenhower considers Latin America alone. Dr. Galbraith considers the United States primarily, with side glances at the rest of the world. Dr. Myrdal, with Sweden ever in the back of his mind, dreads what the loss of American leadership would mean to the other nations that are making an effort at self-government through democratic institutions. Galbraith is— or was when his book appeared five years earlier—determinedly optimistic, but Eisenhower and Myrdal were pretty thoroughly steeped in woe, although neither had surrendered.

So what is an ordinary, unlettered American to think? Perversely, it may be that the very appearance of the three books from such sources will be regarded as offering a partial refutation of their theme. It shows that, despite the much-advertised flight from intelligence, this country continues to incorporate the intellectuals in its political structure. The second Roosevelt's "brain trust" was long regarded as his personal idiosyncrasy; but under the third President after Roosevelt the White House continued to levy upon the university faculties, Kennedy possibly with greater abandon than Roosevelt.

The potential danger in this practice is obvious. There is no place in a democratic system of government for Dr. Dryasdust, the pedant so long and so completely absorbed in books that he has forgotten what men and women are like. To permit that type to frame policies that must be administered by human beings is to court disaster. For Americans the classic example is, of course, John Locke, admittedly one of the greatest of political thinkers as long as he dealt with the abstract but whose draft of a constitution for the Carolinas was so preposterous that even men of the seventeenth century knew better than to make any serious effort to apply it.

On the other hand, the American republic by its sheer magnitude requires, for its successful management, more and more power of abstraction; and it is precisely this power that advanced education is supposed to develop. Thus a seat in the forum is reserved for the professors. Simon Cameron objected to the appointment as Minister to England of the author of *Two Years Before the Mast* because Dana was, in the words of the Pennsylvania boss, "one of those damn literary fellers." Imagination boggles at what he would have said if the appointment had been, say, to the Cabinet.

But that was in the administration of Ulysses S. Grant, when the United States was much smaller and presented its rulers with much simpler problems. Even today the *littérateurs* as department heads are regarded with dubiety; but even the political bosses have to admit that the damned mathematical fellers are indispensable.

Which brings into this discourse an item of political lore as yet less than half mastered, while its implications are far beyond computation. It is the fact that magnitude, quantitative by definition, is also qualitative by a sort of illogic, apprehended but not comprehended by our most acute political philosophers.

That is to say, the typical American as one of nearly two hundred millions is not, cannot be, and ought not to be what he was as one of about three millions in 1776, or would be as one of that same number in 1963. Why? The inquiry must be referred to the masters of the theory of groups, an extremely abstruse branch of higher mathematics. I have been told that they have an answer, and I do not presume to deny it, although it is framed, not in words, but in mathematical symbols beyond my understanding.

I am aware, though, because it has been beaten into my skull by the hammering of events, that exploration of this mystery is one of the unfinished tasks of those Americans who are trying to learn how to be free.

By way of illustration, consider the argument of Dr. Myrdal against Dr. Galbraith. As I said before, they are not at odds on any important part of the factual evidence, and they are in substantial agreement on much of its significance. They both observe that the American social system, like others, tends toward stratification with the passage of time, and both appreciate the powerful influence of the economy on this stratification. Neither blinks the fact that the development has its sinister aspects that under certain circumstances might prove to be premonitions of the failure of this, the greatest—statistically at least—of all human experiments in self-government by free men.

But Galbraith, arguing largely from purely American plus Anglo-American experience, thinks that we should use the economy to correct dangerous tendencies in the social system, while Myrdal, arguing largely from Swedish plus continental European experience, thinks we should use the social system to correct the errors of economics.

To be able to judge between them one needs precisely

the item of information that nobody possesses except, possibly, the group theorists, and they can't tell—or not in terms that any considerable part of the public can understand. This item is the extent, if not exactly, at least to a high degree of accuracy, of the influence of magnitude on political theory and practice. Without that information, one can make only a very rough estimate of the relevance of Swedish experience to American conditions; or even of Anglo-American experience to an Anglo-American system vastly larger than any that has existed heretofore.

That both are relevant admits of no doubt; the question is, how relevant? Contemporary New York could learn many things from Stockholm, and Eisenhower and Kennedy could and did borrow somewhat from the statecraft of William Pitt, but New York city cannot be operated entirely by methods successful in Stockholm, nor can an American President model all his policies on those of Pitt. The fact is obvious, but its quantitative analysis is beyond our skill.

Myrdal is persuasive—shockingly so—in his account of the failure of our current methods of dealing with unemployment. With colorless logic he shows us as extending across the continent what H. M. Caudill, with colorful emotion, showed us* applying to a small section of the Kentucky mountains—that is, a socio-politico-economic system that tends to create a class of people deprived not only of the will but also of the capacity to engage in productive labor.

We are perturbed by the extent to which automation is abolishing jobs, but up to 1963 we had not fully realized its effect in abolishing crafts and skills of many kinds; yet it was glaringly illustrated by the revelation that the railroads were carrying forty thousand men on the trains with nothing to do, since the coming of diesel locomotives had eliminated the need of stoking coal fires. Many of the firemen, probably

*In *Night Comes to the Cumberlands*, 1963.

most of them, had reached the age at which acquiring a new
skill is difficult, if not impossible; and if they were all young
enough to be adaptable, what other jobs are open in which
physical strength is a prime requisite? The harsh truth is
that a large proportion of these men will never work again.

Karl Marx denounced as one of the most vicious of the
evil effects of capitalism—although it was in fact an effect
of technology—the increasing alienation of the worker from
his work. He meant the displacement of craftsmanship by
mass production, blocking the only outlet of creative energy
available to most men. What he would have said of the
alienation of a man not only from his own work but from
all work is beyond conjecture. But, to fit Grover Cleveland's
phrase into a different context, it is a condition that we face
and not a theory.

Myrdal goes at length into the methods devised by Sweden
to cope with this problem. They involve a high degree of
regimentation, which presupposes, of course, a correspondingly high degree of intelligence and integrity in the civil
service. They have been remarkably successful in Sweden,
a small country with a homogeneous population, literate, and
at a relatively high level of political maturity. But that
is far from proving that they would be successful over a
continental expanse in a population of two hundred millions,
polyglot, and including immense masses hardly more advanced politically than the most recent matriculates in the
United Nations.

Without doubt, Swedish experience has some bearing on
our American situation. But how much?

Measurement of such relations with anything remotely
resembling scientific accuracy is, to date, utterly beyond
our powers. Mass psychology is as yet so infantile as hardly
to be called a pseudo-science, and the idea that it can advance at a speed that will keep it abreast of technology can
be entertained only by the wilder compounders of science

fiction. On the face of it, Myrdal's analysis—and, making the necessary allowance for the difference in the angle of approach, Galbraith's also—leaves us practically no room for hope.

And yet . . . "But rabbits can't climb trees," said the Little Boy. "Honey," replied Uncle Remus, "Br'er Rabbit, he 'bleeged ter climb." If you scornfully reject the philosophy of Uncle Remus, then hear Bertrand Russell: "Those who are to lead the world out of its troubles will need courage, hope, and love. Whether they will prevail, I do not know; but, *beyond all reason*, I am unconquerably persuaded that they will."* What's the difference?

Dr. Eisenhower's book appeared a few months ahead of Myrdal's and there is no evidence of any communication between them, but his prolonged examination of Latin America drives him to a conclusion strikingly similar to that of the Swedish savant. He is persuaded that in the southern continent economics must reinforce—"pick up and carry" is a better expression—social reform if economics itself is not to be reduced to an absurdity.

As his brother's envoy, Dr. Eisenhower studied the Latin-American countries intensively, although not continuously, for eight years; and he admits that for rather more than half of that time he was so obsessed by preconceived opinions that he did not grasp the essential truth. That *amour-propre* did not restrain him from making the admission strengthens confidence in the scholar's intellectual integrity and lends weight to his advice.

In sum he agrees, presumably before he ever saw it, with Myrdal's assertion that at present the identical means, and only the identical means, will serve the purposes of both economics and sociology. But Eisenhower refers exclusively to Latin America, Myrdal primarily to the United States.

There is, however, a basic similarity in the two situations.

* Bertrand Russell, *Human Society in Ethics and Politics*, 1955. Italics mine.

The case of Latin America is obviously the more desperate, but the difference is of degree, not of kind. The danger of social and political collapse is more imminent in Latin America—Eisenhower is convinced that collapse is very close indeed in the absence of heroic efforts to stave it off—but in both regions conditions tending to weaken the structure of civilization are present.

Of these, the most sinister is not the cleavage between the classes, but the tendency to harden and perpetuate the status of the submerged classes. Not their present misery, but the fading hope of ever escaping from their misery is the dynamite laid at the foundations of the state. They don't know how to be free, which is bad; and, which is worse, they find nobody—certainly nobody in the existing regimes—capable of teaching them, or apparently much inclined to teach them. Their despair is the active principle productive of berserk rages that explode in one or more of the many forms of totalitarianism.

The question then arises: Is the United States capable of acting as an effective preceptor to those people? Dr. Eisenhower thinks it possible; Dr. Myrdal is more doubtful; but neither exhibits anything like brisk assurance. This leaves the great majority of us, who can lay no claim to detailed and extensive information on the subject, with no firm ground on which to take our stand.

This is a depressing thought, but not quite the counsel of despair. There is a method of coping with a quaking morass. It is to keep moving, to step to a second tussock as the first one sinks; but it is fatiguing, conducive to nervous even sooner than to physical exhaustion, so we don't like it. But, like it or not, it is the only means by which we may reach firm ground if, indeed, any exists.

There is another thought that Americans find disturbing, if rather less depressing. It relates to the traditional difficulty of observing the forest in spite of the trees. In time Dr. Eisenhower perceived the essential truth about Latin America. In time Dr. Myrdal perceived the same truth about the United States. But is the American as reliable an authority on America, or the Swede on Sweden? The doubt is considerable.

I recall, perhaps a bit smugly, one of the rare occasions on which I thought of the right thing to say at the time, not half an hour later. I climbed on an express train bound for New York, and there was Bernard De Voto.

"The very man I wanted to see!" cried Bernie. "Explain Maryland."

"Man, why ask me?" I replied. "I live in Baltimore. If you want Maryland explained, ask a Pennsylvanian or a Virginian."

De Voto snorted, but I was right. As this is written, in 1963, any reasonably well-informed Marylander can explain why Byrd is a Senator from Virginia and perhaps why Scranton is Governor of Pennsylvania; but why Beall is a Senator from Maryland and Tawes its Governor, few of us can tell, not for lack of information, but because we know too many reasons, most of them contradictory.

Of course the tourist—and anyone who has not made a long study of the country he visits is essentially a tourist— is notoriously unreliable because he is almost certain to mistake the insignificant for the essential. On the other hand, excessive familiarity leads to the same end—the outline is obscured by details. The aliens, Tocqueville and Bryce, assuredly taught us much about this country that natives had missed, and Denis Brogan, I believe, is still teaching us. It is a reasonable assumption, then, that Eisenhower may see Latin America and Myrdal the United States more clearly than either sees his native land.

But when each observes in the disparate systems the same

basic flaw, the probability that the flaw is real becomes very high indeed. Americans, North and South, are independent of any foreign control, but they have not yet learned how to be free. Progress toward acquisition of that knowledge, we may hope and believe, continues; but we have yet far to go.

 **XIII**

On Uzzah as a Latter-Day Symbol

IN THE SPRING OF 1963 THE UNITED STATES
Supreme Court decided in favor of the plaintiff a suit
brought by a Baltimore atheist to ban Bible-reading as part
of the opening exercises that public-school children are
obliged to attend.

As a firm believer in complete separation of Church and
State, I read the news with regret. It was not that I ques-
tioned the soundness of the decision. I claim no competence
in law, but in logic I do not see how the Court could have
decided otherwise; my regret was that it had been forced
to rule on such a point, for the litigation was in itself a
distasteful commingling of Church and State, in some measure perverting the judicial into the didactic.

But what can you expect of an atheist? I am impressed
by the wisdom of the sage who observed that an atheist
is nothing but an exceptionally high-proof Calvinist wearing
his religion hind part before. He is as angry with men who
believe in God as the Calvinist is with men who do not. A
genuinely non-religious type does not feel personally injured
by anything that other men believe, as long as they make
no effort to force their belief on him. A man who is emotionally disturbed by the existence of beliefs other than his
own is obviously religious, as far as his neighbors are concerned, for the propagandist is an annoyance whether he

propagates faith or non-faith. Whether the atheist is as rational as the Calvinist is an entirely different question, the answer to which depends upon your own point of view.

From mine, the Calvinist—or the Jansenist, his counterpart in the Roman communion, or the extremely orthodox sectarian in the Jewish—is slightly closer to sanity in that he has certain historical evidence in favor of his tenet. Historically, the existence of God is as palpable as the existence of geometry. Geometry, as every seventh-grade pupil knows, or certainly ought to know, is merely pictured by lines in a textbook or on a blackboard, but it nevertheless exists. More than that, it is as legitimate an object of study in any comprehensive scheme of education.

John Tyndall was so far from being a fundamentalist that in the last quarter of the nineteenth century he was regarded by fundamentalists as the Big Chief Heretic; but it was Tyndall who said of various forms of religion, "It will be wise to recognize them as the forms of a force, mischievous if permitted to intrude on the region of objective knowledge, over which it holds no command, but capable of adding, in the region of poetry and emotion, inward completeness and dignity to man."

Tyndall thus concedes that the idea of God is an existent force capable of producing recognizable effects this side of heaven. True, the "inward completeness and dignity" of a man are impalpable, but they are as perceptible as the magnetic force set up by an electric current passing around a core of soft iron. To deny their existence, and by implication their origin, is as irrational as to hold with Bishop Ussher that the world was created in the year 4004 B.C. The problem of the atheist is to prove that the idea of deity is somehow less real than other abstract concepts—for instance, geometry—and until he has solved that problem the Calvinist has a slightly stronger claim to be taken seriously.

Now the fundamental reason for herding schoolboys into classrooms is to acquaint them with the fact that ideas, although they are invisible, intangible, and imponderable, do, nevertheless, exist. Eliminate that, and you have left no adequate excuse for the process of schooling. It does seem fantastic, then, that in cultivating the power of abstract thinking we must omit examination of the oldest, most widespread, and most influential abstraction known to mankind. The idea of God has been familiar to all societies, at all times, in all parts of the world. But it cannot be examined under the auspices of the state, because every attempt to do so has resulted in mischiefs ranging from intellectual petrifaction to physical murder.

The responsibility for this cannot be laid upon the deists and agnostics; it is the work of the atheists on one hand and of the theocrats on the other. They will not tolerate any approach save their own, hence the state, as representative of all classes, can make no approach at all.

It is a defect in our system of public education, and one so grave that an observer who cannot applaud can yet comprehend the impulse of the Catholics to repudiate the whole thing and to erect a school system of their own. Unfortunately, this is not progress but regress—a return to the theory held by Protestants little more than a hundred years ago that elementary education is properly a familial and congregational, not political, responsibility. In New England the duty of primary education was extended from the home and the church to the town; but Harvard and Yale were church schools, while William and Mary had the curious distinction of being both—a church school but sponsored by the royal family. In Georgia and North Carolina higher education was seen as a state responsibility. Both set up state universities in the eighteenth century, but neither took over the elementary schools.

In recent years the Catholics have been learning what Horace Mann taught the Protestants beginning about 1837, namely, that the magnitude of the task is beyond the strength of the church and the home. Purely religious training they can manage, but the general education now required in order to hold even a minor job is too costly to be supplied by any authority short of one that has power to tax all property and all persons—that is to say, the government. Accordingly, we are driven to the device, unsatisfactory even if reluctantly sanctioned by the Supreme Court, of splitting off a segment of what should not be divided, leaving in the hands of the home and the church an important part of general education. It is the best we can do, but it is essentially a police measure adopted, not for its intrinsic merit, but for the purpose of discouraging breaches of the peace.

The real necessity of the device was revealed by the outburst of indignation following the Bible-reading decision. It is a safe guess that at least ten thousand Letters to the Editor all over the country asserted that the Supreme Court had expelled God from the public schools. In Baltimore one American Legion post adopted a resolution—rejected, I hasten to add, by the state convention—demanding impeachment of eight of the Justices for this high crime and misdemeanor. One—Stewart, I believe—was omitted from the list because it was reported that he keeps a Bible in his desk. Evidently, in the Legionnaires' opinion, a Bible is equal in power to Ulysses' sprig of moly as a protection against sorcery.

What an admission is this clamor! In the estimation of these people God, it seems, is no match for the Supreme Court. They claim that He is great, but not great enough to take care of Himself without the assistance of politicians, elected or appointed, in Washington! To the agnostic, of course, these are the skeptics, rather than those who are doubtful of the verbal inspiration of the Scriptures; and to the deist—twentieth century, not eighteenth—they appear to be trying to hold contradictory views.

So it appears to me; but I doubt that it lies in my mouth to criticize them on that score, because in matters of exegesis I hold some contradictory opinions myself. I am inclined to believe, for instance, that the story of Uzzah is both historically and symbolically true; but I am pretty sure that a strict Calvinist would condemn my view as inconsistent and heretical.

King David is said to have charged Uzzah and his brother with the duty of driving the cart that was to bring the sacrosanct Ark of the Covenant from its temporary resting place to the King's house, and it is written: "When they came to Nachon's threshing-floor, Uzzah put forth his hand to the ark of God, and took hold of it; for the oxen shook it. And the anger of the Lord was kindled against Uzzah; and God smote him there for his error; and there he died by the ark of God."*

I see no reason to doubt that this story is historical fact. Hypertension and thromboses are not modern inventions of the medical faculty, but their correct diagnosis is. So if Uzzah suffered a stroke or a coronary occlusion a moment after steadying the Ark, the supposition that God smote him, since no man had done so, was not unreasonable in itself. The irrational element enters with the statement (verse 8) that the King "was displeased because the Lord had made a breach upon Uzzah," yet David, surely the worse offender, remained unsmitten; hence the deduction that the Lord deliberately smote Uzzah is open to doubt. But from the literalist's point of view that is heresy.

Yet if the Lord did smite the man, why does He now

*II Samuel 6:6–7. In I Chronicles 13:9 the story is repeated with the variation, "the oxen stumbled."

withhold his hand from those who presume to prop up religion with a policeman's club? If the tale of Uzzah is symbolically as well as historically true, it is logical to suppose that those who insist that the state must steady the Ark are inviting condign punishment.

As self-contradictorily, perhaps, as any fundamentalist, I cling to two apparently inconsistent beliefs: first, that Uzzah died of natural causes and, second, that his death nevertheless has a symbolical significance applicable to our times. David's unpunished displeasure with the Lord supports the first view, and the historical record of Church-State relations supports the second, for I believe that modern trespassers are smitten, part of their punishment being that they do not realize it.

Jefferson's "wall of separation" between Church and State applied, in the beginning, strictly to federal relations. Eventually, all the states adopted the same policy, but not for some time after adoption of the Constitution. For one, I believe that making church membership and church support entirely voluntary had no effect whatever on religion; but under that policy church membership has flourished so prodigiously that today 52 per cent of all Americans are affiliated with some organized religious body.

My doubt that this has much to do with religion, one way or the other, is based on the fact that long years ago, while I was still a resident of North Carolina, church membership in that state reached 51 per cent. But public jubilation over the figure died suddenly when unregenerate newspaper reporters discovered that of the inmates of the state penitentiary 56 per cent claimed to be church members.

Yet while one may strongly suspect that the truly religious Americans number materially less than 52 per cent of the population, the supposition that religion as a social force has vanished is preposterous. To take the most crass of all measurements, the American people do not spend—voluntarily, mind you—a matter of three billion dollars a year to support a program that they consider without force or effect. But why labor the point? Any man unaware of the influence of religion on the life of the nation is so imperceptive as to be beyond the reach of argument.

It may be contended with some plausibility, of course, that in no Christian nation is religion anything like the effective social and political force that it is among the heathen, especially among the Moslems, Hindus, and Buddhists. Self-immolation in testimony to the faith, at least by fire, is practically unheard of among Americans, and not since the butchery of the Mormons have we been more than mildly addicted to lynching in the name of the Lord. Character assassination, to be sure, is a different story, as witness the attribution of moral turpitude to the eight Justices of the Supreme Court who do not habitually carry a Bible. But the victims of that kind of thing have a disconcerting way of surviving, and even thriving under attack.

The fact that Christianity is less bloodthirsty than it once was, and very much less so than any other faith of comparable extent, is not persuasive evidence of its weakening as an influence upon our social and political system. It is easy to believe the contrary—that under the policy of separation of Church and State it has grown stronger than it was at the time of adoption of the Constitution, when three fourths or more of the people were not church members. Deprived of such instruments of propaganda as the jail, the pillory, and the gallows of old Salem, it has made more effective use of moral suasion than it ever did of physical force.

Acceptance of this estimate of the current situation necessitates acceptance of religion as a powerful influence upon our way of life. It follows that it is a proper subject of study in any school that purports to give a general education. It

should begin where reading, writing, and arithmetic begin
and should continue as far as the student goes in mathematics, history, and languages. Ideally, the kindergartener
and the candidate for the Ph.D. should both be capable of
taking an oral in religion, different only in the difficulty of
the questions.

But it is flatly impossible as long as education remains a
function of the state; and it will remain a function as long
as it it too heavy a burden for home and church to carry.

It was not a political function at the time the Constitution
was written. At that time it was not, period. The concepts
of universal education had then permeated only a few minds
of advanced thinkers, such as Jefferson and—astonishingly to
most Americans—the original Du Pont de Nemours. The
idea that everybody must learn to read and write was engendered by the Industrial Revolution, not the political one.

Yet when it arrived, it proved assimilable, although with
difficulty; and that was true because members of the Convention of 1787 were so sharply aware that their work was
largely guesswork. Representative democracy was an un-
proved theory, a hypothesis not yet tested on any extensive
scale; it followed that in erecting this theory into a system
of government it was only common sense to allow a wide
margin for error that was more than possible, that was
highly probable. Thus whenever they could they excluded
problems known to be particularly thorny from the purview
of the federal government. Religion they knew to be the
thorniest of all, so they ruled it out as rigidly as the English
language would permit. The "free exercise" of religion was
neither to be established nor prohibited by law; Congress
was to "make no law" concerning it.

The Supreme Court has ruled that what Congress can't
do is prohibited to all other lawmaking bodies, down to and
including school boards. There shall simply be no law about

it; and since schools cannot be operated without rules, a subject on which no rules can be made must be omitted from the work of the school.

This was the most hateful of all possible policies in the eyes of all fanatics of all sects, which attests its wisdom, for to incur the hatred of fanatics is routine procedure in the exercise of freedom. The genuine fanatic is possessed of the slave mentality that dreams of mastery but can endure servitude; what it finds intolerable is liberty. The fanatical fundamentalist Protestant could be relatively happy under an establishment of Anglicanism or even Catholicism, for an establishment of any kind would enable him to canalize and thereby intensify the hate by which he lives and which, under the condition of religious freedom, spreads so widely as to become shallow and ineffective.

That this was clear to the Founding Fathers is debatable, but it is certain that they were acutely aware of the experimental nature of their work. They were laying foundations, and the requisite in that operation is to make them sturdy enough to bear the weight of any imaginable superstructure that sane men would erect upon them.

The wiser among their successors have been satisfied to make sure that their own work rests squarely on the foundations, so that it may support the additions of those who will come after them. But almost every subsequent generation has been afflicted by persons who conceive it their God-given function to set the highest of the finials in place, concluding the great experiment; and these, of course, must be torn off by the next generation with great labor and loss.

Perhaps it is just this loss of the sense of the experimental, the tentative, that constitutes the "Degradation of the Democratic Dogma" so vividly apparent to Henry and Brooks Adams. "We are the people and wisdom shall die with us" has been the faith of every King of Fools from Ozymandias to Hitler; and it is the basis of half the legislation introduced in Congress every day. Fortunately, few of the bills introduced ever come to a vote, and still fewer pass, so the amount of such legislation on the statute books, although alarming, has not yet proved fatal.

Here, then, is an element of our democratic structure—an ell, a bay, a transept, a chapel, name it as you will, but essential to the symmetry and harmony of the whole design —so far from completion that as yet it has hardly risen above the foundation. But work upon it has been brought to a halt by a jurisdictional dispute among fanatics of all varieties.

The basis of my regret that the Bible is excluded from the classroom is not entirely theological or pedagogical. In part it is professional. I believe that the school children lose on both counts, but I know that the professional writer loses when his audience is no longer familiar with the Bible, especially the King James Version.

I remember a lament by the late H. L. Mencken, certainly no religious fanatic, bearing on this point. The then President of the United States, perplexed by some current proposal, had summoned a group of reputed wise men to advise him. Mencken wished to convey the idea that he took a dim view of the wisdom of the group and of the value of their advice; so he remarked that the President had "called in the Chaldeans and soothsayers." He was flooded with letters asking who the Chaldeans might be, for the Book of Daniel was apparently unknown to his readers.

The Biblical allusion is a variety of shorthand, compressing not words but a whole complex of ideas into a stroke. It is no small convenience to be able to describe a man as a Jehu without having to add that "he driveth furiously," or as an Agag without explaining that he "walked delicately." Where shall we find a substitute for Iscariot as the supreme epithet? Shaw summarized a long play in three words when he wrote *Back to Methuselah*, but not for a man who had never seen Genesis 5:27. "She brought forth butter in a lordly dish," as a prelude to sudden, violent death, perhaps always was a bit esoteric, but in my youth "a Song of Deborah," from which the line comes, would have been widely understood as meaning a paean more vindictive, if possible, than "The Battle Hymn of the Republic."

The clichés, however, were at best mere time-savers. A far greater loss is general appreciation of the texture of the language, its rhythms, its balanced antitheses, its delicate poetry and stunning anathemas, nowhere more perfectly expressed than in the King James Version, published in 1611, just after English literature as an art form had culminated in Shakespeare. Worst of all is loss of understanding of the basis of the philosophy of the past two thousand years.

> Clement, Augustin, Origen,
> Burnt brightlier toward their setting day,

but they burn dimly indeed for the man without the faintest notion of the source of their ideas.

This is, I repeat, a strictly professional plaint, no doubt frivolous by comparison with the lofty ethical code and the broadened intellectual horizon that the Bible offers school children, but it happens to touch me sharply. In the course of my life's work as a writer of—ostensibly—non-fiction I have worn out three Bibles and the fourth is beginning to look shabby, as is my second copy of Cruden's *Concordance*. The Bibles are all King James, of course. I have several modern revised versions, but they stand on my bookshelves practically as good as new. I have yet to be able to use the language of any revision to put real thunder into, say, denunciation of a crooked politician. But the King James . . . listen, man: "Judgment will I lay to the line and righteousness to the plummet. And your covenant with death shall be

disannulled, and your agreement with hell shall not stand."
Beat that for a comment on a City Hall character who, for a
price, has been giving his official OK to some jerry-builder's
shoddy work!

Study of religion is most certainly an integral part of
anything fit to be called general education. But it is as true
beyond doubt as anything in history that if the state undertakes to teach it the outcome will be a travesty of religion
and the disruption of the state. Carried to an extreme, it
will mean not holiness but bloodshed. There is a gaping
hole in our democratic structure, and how it is to be filled
I do not know. It is shocking evidence of how incomplete
is our knowledge of how to be free.

XIV

On Calling Spirits from
the Vasty Deep

IN THE SUMMER OF 1963 THE AMERICAN LIBRARY
Association published a brochure of thirty-two pages under
the title "Expanding Population in a Shrinking World." Its
author was Dr. Marston Bates, a biologist and demographer
of the University of Michigan, and its aim was, first, to
summarize the known facts and, second, to recommend a
dozen authoritative books treating the subject in greater
detail.

I read it all, conscious that in so doing I was furnishing
support to Lippmann's observation of many years ago that
people are not interested in their interests. He meant that
the chambermaid and the houseboy, if such creatures still
exist, will ignore a newspaper column explaining the city's
efforts, usually vigorous and sometimes intelligent, to provide decent low-cost housing for chambermaids and houseboys, but will read avidly five columns devoted to the
Profumo scandal although, far from affecting them, it did
not even happen in their own country.

All hands agree that the effects of the population explosion will become critical not earlier than the year 2000,
probably a generation or two beyond that date. Now the
chance that I shall have a direct, personal interest in anything that happens in the year 2000 is so remote that it
may be disregarded. Yet I read about it.

Nor is there any singularity in that, as the appearance of the pamphlet proves. The American Library Association is a national organization that does not cater to parochial tastes. It is, furthermore, an organization of public libraries—"public" in this connection meaning any library not restricted to the use of the owner and his friends—and the public library is the acme of neutralism, never inciting controversy, and taking note of its existence only when it has grown too important to be ignored.

Thus publication of the pamphlet under such auspices is conclusive proof that very large numbers of Americans are very much interested in a problem that will become acute only when their grandchildren, more likely their great-grandchildren will bear responsibility for public policy.

This is not a childish attitude; on the contrary, it would seem to be rather impressive evidence of an approach to political maturity. In theory, now is the time when a disastrous expansion of population could be prevented. Thus our interest in the problem evinces some consciousness of our situation as participants in a continuing process, links in a chain that as far as we know is endless, with the corollary that our quality will inevitably affect an indeterminate future.

In the strictly scientific aspects of the current discussion, whether the science be biology, sociology, agronomy, or economics, my interest is languid, first, because scientific questions are the province of scientists and, second, because none of the disciplines has as yet come up with a suggested solution broad enough and plausible enough to be impressive. Perhaps posterity is destined to harvest the sea and compete with the whales for plankton, or perhaps it will discover the secret of chlorophyll and subsist upon sunlight. Since I am not called on to do anything about either, I am indifferent to both.

What comes close enough to create a slight disturbance of my equanimity is the insistence of sociologists that the key to the problem is in the hands of the living generation, which ought to attempt a solution with the inadequate information that we now possess rather than idly wait upon some unpredictable advance in chemotherapy, physiotherapy, orthopraxis, or whatever, to give us an answer that is not only correct but applicable to vast numbers of people. The implication is that the problem is as much philosophical as scientific, and that excuses nobody, for it is the thinking of great numbers that shapes the dominant philosophy of any society.

It has not escaped the attention of the savants that the sites of the population explosion are areas characterized by low income, high illiteracy, and widespread hunger. They have duly noted that as soon as industrialization produces a material increase in per capita income the birth rate drops in the area affected. From this they have deduced that the nutritional factor has an important influence on both the primitive cultural level and the exceptional human fertility of these regions; hence elimination of ignorance and hunger offers the most promising avenue of approach to prevention of disastrous overpopulation.

I can pick no flaw in this reasoning; therefore I am not disposed to challenge the conclusion. A change in the environment obviously produces gross effects very difficult to produce through individual action. But as a bystander who has been bystanding longer than 85 per cent of the population, I venture the opinion that the scientists are neglecting a factor that may possibly be as important as nutrition in reducing excessive fertility. This is distraction.

The regions in which the increase of population is most rapid do have in common the two characteristics of ignorance and hunger. But they also have a third—boredom. If

any man on earth lives a duller life than that of a Bolivian
Indian peasant, it must be a Chinese coolie. Even a Hindu
farmer in the middle of the subcontinent probably has an
edge on the Bolivian, if only by a hairsbreadth. No doubt
the increased caloric intake resulting from industrialization
is part of the explanation of a falling birth rate; but new
sights, new sounds, new neighbors, and new excitements also
accompany industrialization and may also play a part.

Thirty years ago, when lynching was still endemic in this
country, Mencken proffered a suggestion for stamping it
out that, like many of his most brilliant ideas, was mistaken
for farce. His specific for the disease of mob murder was
brass bands. Organize one in every forlorn backwoods com-
munity and it would break the intolerable monotony that in
his opinion was one of the most potent causes of outbreaks
of bestial ferocity.

There is this much to support his view: the subsidence
of lynching has proceeded *pari passu* with removal of the
isolation that for generations had made the lives of rural
dwellers in many parts of America so drab and dull that the
incidence of insanity among farmers' wives was appalling.

It may be objected that the problem under consideration
is the reverse of lynching—not the blind destruction, but the
blind generation, of life. Perhaps an answer to that is the
fact that of all the fauna spawned by Mother Earth the
fiercest by long odds is the white man. It is therefore logical
enough that when the tedium of his life becomes intolerable
his rebellion against it should be marked by a ferocity un-
equaled among milder breeds—pogroms in Russia, lynchings in America, the two countries in which rural life was
most often isolated and inexpressibly dull.

It is reasonable to assume that less bloodthirsty strains
would find release in milder activities, but the need for
release of some kind is universal. If sexual play is the only

form of amusement readily available, as it is among illiterate and desperately poor people, what else could be expected but a high birth rate?

The point is worth considering when the effects of the population explosion are plainly nearing the danger line. Theoretically at least, it adds to education and industralization a third weapon against the menace, to wit, distraction. Furthermore, it is a weapon that can be employed without collision with our established mores and without any suggestion of moral usurpation.

There is a valid objection to propaganda in favor of birth control when agencies of the United States government do the propagandizing, but it is not based on religious dogma or silly prudery. In rests, rather, upon a decent refusal to attribute to ourselves a moral superiority to other nations and other races.

It applies exclusively to official action, for the reason that official action is supposed to be impersonal. When an individual deals with another individual, the relation is quite different. For one American to offer contraceptive information to one Chinese who has already begotten fourteen children may be a friendly act motivated only by concern for the welfare of the man and his family.

But for the United States government to suggest to the Chinese people generally that they apply what we have learned about reducing the birth rate admits of but one interpretation, namely, that in American official opinion there are already too many Chinese. To say that Ah Sin should repress his philoprogenitive impulse because he can't support the children he already has is no reflection on the Chinese race; but an assertion that there are too many Chinese most certainly is.

The work that American medical science has done in backward regions of the world is unquestionably one of the finest contributions to civilization made by this country. It can be reasonably claimed, too, that the preventive greatly exceeds in importance the clinical part of this work—that in preaching everywhere the principles of immunology, sanitation, and hygiene the American doctor abroad has done more for the world than he could possibly do by treatment of patients.

It is true that this strictly scientific work arouses a certain amount of hostility because it comes into collision with superstition. The shamans, witches, and warlocks resent being displaced; but theirs is a class, not a racial, resentment and it can be dealt with by their own people. But birth control is sociology, not medicine, except as the doctors can detect and condemn dangerous methods. Medical men, therefore, should leave sociology to the sociologists.

On the other hand, if any foreign nation, through its own lawful government, asks for such information as American medical science possesses, on this or any other problem, it is a reversion to barbarism to deny it. The discoveries of science, especially biological science, are the common property of mankind and should be made available to anyone who needs them.

Then for any department of our government, Congress included, to decree than an American doctor abroad, because he is paid out of tax money, shall be forbidden to disseminate any medical knowledge that he has acquired is equally an act of moral usurpation. The fact that some states of this Union do restrict medical practitioners for sectarian or sumptuary reasons is no excuse for thrusting our peculiar view on other people. To do so is arrogance.

It is arrogance in any people, but in the case of the American people it is more—it is a repudiation of their own professed faith. The great state papers that by general agreement contain the distillation of the American idea of government—the Declaration, the Constitution, the Farewell Address, *The Federalist*, the inaugurals of Jefferson and Lincoln, the Gettysburg Address—are all couched in simple language. Anyone capable of reading an ordinary newspaper can understand what they say. To understand all that they mean is, of course, a different matter; but we can approach that understanding only by careful study of what they say.

Their language leaves no doubt that each of these documents is based on the assumption that the American people are committed to the theory that it is entirely right and proper that other peoples should live. I am aware that within the past twenty years this interpretation has been sternly challenged, and not by any geographically restricted group. In every section of the country there are persons who seem to be driven into frenzy by bare mention of the word "coexistence," and the frenzy is doubled in intensity if the word is preceded by "peaceful." Yet, since war involves killing, coexistence without peace is obviously a contradiction in terms.

The inescapable inference is that these persons do not admit any commitment to the theory that other peoples have an inalienable right to life. Their right is conditional. It is alienable unless they conform, at least to a minimal extent, to the American scale of human values.

No pacifist, I agree that if their non-conformity to our set of values goes the length of attempting to kill us, then the theory of Americanism does not imply an obligation to coexist with them, and we may butcher them with complete consistency. But there is a sharp, clear line between proclaiming the opinion that we ought not to be allowed to live and making an overt attempt to kill us, as the Japanese did in 1941. But until they cross that line, any non-American people have a right to live, and it is a flat negation of Americanism to say otherwise.

But while this seems to be crystal-clear, fog begins to enshroud the question when it is a matter, not of denying the right of other people to exist, but of persuading them not to exercise that right. Advocacy of contraception is persuasion toward non-existence. Theodore Roosevelt was talking arrant nonsense when he called it "race suicide" because the opposite course is not only race suicide but, by forcing attempts at conquest, is also an invitation to mass murder. But there is no denying that some very fine distinctions are involved, one being that between official and non-official advocacy, which is the distinction between intrusion and assistance.

All of which gives rise to a strong suspicion that much of the talk about how to avoid a population explosion is based upon a false premise, to wit, the delusion that the United States at its present cultural level is capable of making a wise decision relative to this problem. Evidence is lacking that we, as a people, have made sufficient progress toward mastering the art of self-government to be competent to advise others in a matter closely related to their national—or should one say tribal?—existence.

Nor should we fail to take into account the ever-present chance that at the critical moment we shall have no choice or voice in the matter. Extreme pressure of population on the means of subsistence may result in mass hysteria that will engulf reason in the overpopulated countries and cause them to rush upon their own destruction. This was certainly one component of the suicidal policy of Japan.

In any sane view this would be little preferable to ultimate disaster, for it would drive us to perpetration of such a holocaust as history has not yet had the dreadful duty of recording. If the critical moment comes at or near the year 2000, it is almost a certainty that our technology will still be well in advance of that of our assailants, so that, however badly hurt, we should still be able to retaliate strongly. Nor is it likely that the ingrained ferocity of the white man will have abated materially in a matter of forty years. Add, then, the stimulus of severe fright, and it is all but a foregone conclusion that we should flail the world with a storm of unimaginable horrors.

It is a deed that would mingle the wine of victory with gall and wormwood, for while we might have solved the problem of overpopulation for a long time, it would have been at the price of a reversion to the moral level of the darkest of the Dark Ages. Out of that pit it would take us generations, probably centuries, to climb back to our present level, which, God knows, is low enough.

I have never been one of those Americans who seem to be hag-ridden by guilt over Hiroshima. Given the state of mind of the Japanese high command on August 6, 1945, I believe that Hiroshima actually saved more Japanese lives than it destroyed—to say nothing of our own prospective losses. But I confess that I am appalled by the prospect of repeating Hiroshima *n* times, all over the earth. It would mean that the great experiment undertaken in 1776 had produced, not a beacon, but a death-light for mankind. Could failure be more complete?

There is no shadow of doubt that the threat of a population explosion is serious, even if it still lies beyond the horizon of the living generation. Therefore I am inclined to snatch at any straw. Brass bands? By all means, if the trio, industrialization, nutrition, and diversion, by changing the environment can effect the purpose. For that would relieve us of the necessity of summoning from the vasty deep the two dread spirits of moral arrogance and physical carnage. "But will they come," quoth Hotspur, "when you do call for them?" They most certainly will, usually one close behind the other, or all history is a liar.

Yet, in discoursing on this theme, any man of mature years illustrates Lippmann's dictum that we are interested in things that do not affect our own interests. Age enables us to repeat with a certain insouciance,

> And ye, red-lipped and smooth-browed; list,
> Gentlemen,
> Much is there waits you we have missed;

perchance including triumphs we have not won that will compensate for defeats we have suffered. Who knows? At this moment there may be in library or laboratory some anonymous youth in whose brain is already stirring the idea that will exorcise the demon by means unguessed by us. However, if he fails I shall be unperturbed; for if the population explosion reaches the critical point at or near A.D. 2000, in the course of nature it is reasonably certain that I shall not be around to be hoist with that petard.

 **XV**

On Fostering a Redheaded Stepchild

IN THE SUMMER OF 1963 I HAD THE UNUSUAL experience of chatting with one who had then a claim—not exclusive, but a fair claim—to be considered the most frustrated man on earth. This was Dr. Frank Porter Graham, United Nations mediator between India and Pakistan in the matter of Kashmir. At the start mediation was fairly successful. A ceasc-fire was managed, and a *modus vivendi* along the line was established; optimists looked forward to a durable peace under the auspices of the United Nations.

But then the Russians took a hand. The Chinese took a hand. The Egyptians took a hand. Our State Department and the British Foreign Office, of course, had been right in the middle of things from the beginning. The United Nations was thrust into the background and old-style diplomacy went into operation to produce old-style results. Kashmir is now recognized as an international powder keg, liable to blow at any minute.

I had not seen Dr. Graham previously for quite a long time, but I had noted occasional press references to him, some of them unflattering. Certain Pakistani leaders were quoted as describing him as pro-India. Certain Indian leaders were as certain that he was pro-Pakistan. In Washington I had encountered State Department personnel—but underlings, I hasten to say, never the Secretary—who darkly hinted that he was in effect an agent of Soviet Russia, while the Russian press openly charged that he was an agent of capitalistic imperialism, Wall Street, and the Pentagon.

Rashly, perhaps, I said to him, "If you were in fact the agent of all these interests at the same time you would be the worst split personality in the annals of psychiatry, which is plainly not the case. How, then, did you contrive to get in bad with everybody?"

"Perfectly naturally," he replied. "You see, I am actually an agent of none of the four, but of a fifth party, the United Nations. Its primary interest is the four million people living in Kashmir, who have nobody else to put their interest first. But a basic tenet of nationalism is 'He who is not for us is against us,' and there you are."

There, indeed, we are, and there we have been, time out of mind. In the nature of the case the United Nations is bound to be the redheaded stepchild of all the world, and its agents, exactly in measure as they are honest, are bound to be regarded as dishonest. As long as every man's hand is against Ishmael, it will be assumed that his hand is against every man. The evidence that Ishmael's intentions are strictly honorable will be brushed aside or cited as proof of his deceitfulness.

So it has been in the past, so it is now, and it takes resolution, not to say recklessness, to refuse to join those who confidently add, so it will be forevermore. The United Nations is an instrumentality designed to put some restraint on international greed, mendacity, and deceit; hence it is bound to be hateful to the rulers of the earth, for greed, mendacity, and deceit are princely virtues, as all the world has known since Machiavelli let the cat out of the bag. This is why honest men have ever regarded government as an unfortunate necessity and Samuel Johnson remarked that "patriotism is the last refuge of a scoundrel."

Thus to predict that the United Nations will succeed is to predict that the Machiavellian Prince will be displaced and succeeded by honest men, which is unblushing idealism. Yet it is historical fact that this idea has been adumbrated by some extremely practical characters and apparently has increased rather than diminished in potency. Alexander the Great may have been entirely alone in his dream of *Homonoia,* the Concord of Mankind. Marcus Aurelius may have been singular in observing that "we are born for co-operation, as are the feet, the hands, the eyelids, and the upper and lower jaws." The Duc de Sully may have been unable to sell Henri Quatre on the *Grand Dessein,* but at least he induced the King to listen. Grotius at times was taken quite seriously by quite a few practical politicians. Woodrow Wilson almost summoned a majority to the support of the League of Nations, and F. D. Roosevelt did align a working majority behind the United Nations. It may be plausibly argued, then, that the really reckless prediction is a prediction that the immemorial loneliness of the advocates of Concord will continue indefinitely.

Unfortunately, this is no guarantee of the survival of the United Nations. The perdurability of an idea does not attach to the institutions that from time to time embody it. Occasionally the United Nations has imposed some small restraint upon the ferocity of human greed, and this has arrayed the stupendous power of avarice against it; but it has not effectively chained the tiger, and its failure to do so has impelled many Tired Liberals to abandon it. Perhaps within a few years it may go the way of the League of Nations.

One might predict that outcome with confidence if the only hope of its survival rested upon Plato's dictum that good government will be attained only when philosophers become kings, or kings philosophers. The rise, if any, in the general level of morality among mankind in the latter half of history, say in the last three thousand years, has been so slight that none of our available instruments is capable of measuring it; but the softening of manners is the story of civilization. Man may be no better than he was when he painted the caves of Aurignac and Mas d'Azil; but that he behaves better is attested by the mere fact that he increased and multiplied and replenished the earth. If he had remained in a state of complete savagery he would still be among the rarest of the mammals.

It is a mistake, therefore, to write off the United Nations' chance of survival merely because it is conditioned on a marked increase of tolerance, of foresight, and of accurate judgment, which is to say, an advance in political maturity in the world at large. An advance is probable, because it is being forced. But it is equally a mistake to assume that the future of the United Nations is assured, because the advance may be too slow to save it.

Within the time covered by recorded history, civilization, according to Toynbee, has collapsed fifteen times and been partially paralyzed five more. It is information of interest to statisticians, no doubt, but to the ordinary voter the relevant point is that civilization, like Banquo "with twenty mortal murders on [its] crown," still walks, indeed, still increases in potency and the length of its reach. It is chillingly indifferent to its institutions; theocracy, autocracy, democracy, *polis*, church, state, commune rise, flourish, and wither, to the consternation of men who have pinned their faith to any institution, mistaking the

> embodiment
> Of everything that's excellent

for the excellence itself. Thus philosophy is reduced to weeping and civilization pursues its way through an incessant din of threnodies.

Tolerance, judgment, and foresight are political virtues. Hence if the success or even the survival of the United Nations depends upon their steady and fairly rapid increase, it would seem that it depends upon the prospect that men will steadily become more virtuous; and that prospect cannot be called brilliant. This is the basis of the pessimism of those who contend that the idea behind the United Nations was preposterous from the start because it is in direct opposition to human nature.

They have a case, but it is not quite perfect. Grant, for the sake of argument, that organization of the nations to establish and maintain permanent peace implies patience, sacrifice, and magnanimity to a degree not consonant with what we know of human nature, there is still a question. Is it consonant with animal nature, which, as most of us believe, antedates and underlies human nature?

Genus *Homo*, including the species *sapiens*, is one of a number of genera with the character called gregariousness. All are capable of making adjustments required by this character, and *Homo sapiens* differs from the rest only in that his adjustments are far more elaborate and more rapid than those of any other animal. He has progressed so far that he is capable occasionally of foreseeing the necessity of adjusting before it becomes desperately urgent; and this capacity, highly developed, becomes the art of government. It follows that to assure man's dexterity in this art it is not necessary that he should become more virtuous, in which his progression is dubious, but merely that he should become more numerous, which he certainly has done.

Numerical increase of any species of social animal therefore necessitates either constant development of the social organization or a reversal of the numerical increase; and such reversal may reasonably be expected to result in an arrest or a deterioration of the social organization. This expectation is borne out by the historical record of mankind; war, pestilence, and famine on a massive scale have ever been destructive of civilization.

It is apparent, then, that three, and only three, possible directions are open to the trend of history in the immediate future—"immediate" meaning, in this connection, the remainder of this century and perhaps part of the next. The three possibilities are (1) that the United Nations will be steadily and fairly rapidly improved as a governmental system covering the world, or (2) that it will be replaced by an organization of the same general type but of higher efficiency, or (3) that the population of the earth will be reduced by the destruction of a considerable proportion of the total. This might be effected by hunger and disease, but war is much more rapid, and the introduction of nuclear weapons has made it so enormously more efficient that it is likely to be the preferred agency.

That is, however, a matter of small moment, since depopulation by any of the three agencies would involve the destruction of Western civilization, followed by a period, presumably of some centuries, of painful effort to construct another.

Sanity, of course, dictates the choice of either (1) or (2)—either improvement or replacement of the United Nations. It is the function of United Nations men to carry out (1), the policy of improvement, and this function imposes upon them an intellectual and moral solitude that Robinson Crusoe never imagined. This probably does not apply on the lower levels. Minor U.N. functionaries, on the contrary, perhaps enjoy greater security and closer companionship in the organization than they did at home. But from the level of Dr. Graham up to that of U Thant it does apply, and with especial force to the heads of the national delegations.

Consider, for example, the Hon. Adlai E. Stevenson, in

1963 the top United States representative at the United Nations. Mr. Stevenson is a man whom I have always admired but never envied. It seems to me that the pillory in seventeenth-century Salem must have been a rather more comfortable seat than the chair of the Governor of Illinois when Stevenson occupied it; and the extravagance of the Democratic party in sacrificing him as a burnt offering on the altar of frenzied hero worship is usually accounted his personal tragedy. That, I presume to doubt. I am inclined to think, on the contrary, that Stevenson's one streak of luck was being pitted not against a Republican, any of whom he could have beaten, but against five stars that can be beaten only by six stars, and no man legitimately wears six. But for that fortunate circumstance he would have had to preside over the country during one of its recurrent spells of moral and intellectual torpor. It would have maddened him. It might have killed him.

But being translated to the United Nations in the decade of the Sixties was no felicitous escape. Stevenson's predecessor, Lodge the Younger, although a man of exceptional emotional stability, emerged from the experience subdued, not to say shaken; and the strain increased steadily during the following years.

One reason for this is perfectly plain. It is the difficulty of communication. But there is another, which pious commentators refuse to admit exists and even the unregenerate tend to slur over because its acridity is rather too much for the mildly cynical. It is the fact that perhaps one American out of eight, a strong minority, is consciously or unconsciously a warmonger. The conscious ones are for war because they make money out of it; the more numerous ones are for it because they enjoy it. They deny it furiously, of course, but a great many Americans, especially women, had the time of their lives from 1941 to 1945. Boredom was banished. Every

individual able to stand up and feed a machine was besought
to enter the war industries; and healthy women as never
before found their pockets full of money and their lives full
of excitement, importance, and freedom. Of course they
enjoyed it.

At a guess, this minority may be less than 12½ per cent,
but its lungs are strong out of all proportion to its numbers,
and its hatred of the United Nations is logical and probably
irremovable.

The other reason, however, is more important both because it affects more people and because it is, in theory
at least, not immutable. Lack of communication is not restricted to any small group, but is widely pervasive. It
is due to the lag of our political thinking behind the pace of
world politics, and in theory that lag can be closed. But as
things stand now, the United Nations man as a matter of
daily routine deals with questions a large proportion of
which are beyond the purview of the typical American
citizen.

The natural result is that the United Nations man regularly talks what to millions of his fellow Americans seems
to be nonsense. Not many of us have attained the attitude of
the natural scientist, who knows that if he puts a question
to nature and gets an idiotic answer the inescapable inference is either that his instruments are inaccurate or the
question itself was idiotic. For instance, if we put to the
United Nations the question, "Why not immediately establish the initiative, referendum, and recall in Laos?" and
get what seems to us a damfool answer, we deserve it for
asking a damfool question.

But our representative, of course, is estopped from explaining this. The American public is his boss and he can't
accuse the boss of idiocy if he hopes to stay on the job.
Out of the complex of relations, for the most part utterly

unknown to Americans, with which the Assembly and Security Council deal regularly, constantly come answers bearing no apparent relation to known facts. In such a case the natural assumption of the ordinary newspaper reader is not that there is a vast body of unknown facts to which the answer bears a completely logical relation, but that someone, presumably our man, has asked a fool question; and there is nothing for our man to do except hunch his shoulders and take the storm of criticism that follows.

Why do they do it? To the disengaged bystander that question is more interesting than any of the problems being debated in the Assembly. There is nothing unique about Graham and Stevenson. Their names happen to be the two that first come to this observer's mind, but as much might be said of a small army of men of first-rate ability drawn from more than a hundred nations; their job is laborious, frustrating, vulnerable, and in some cases physically dangerous—not to our men, but delegates from some of the more immature and turbulent nations actually risk jail or the gallows. Yet they stick to it.

Cynicism, of course, can supply various motives more or less discreditable—vanity, ambition, rivalry, service of a particular personal or national interest, hope of sabotage. Some of these undoubtedly figure, and all of them may enter the equation from time to time. But it is hard to believe that so many men, of so many and such various types, could be dominated by these for so long a time. The one motive that can be expected to stir men of all types at all times is the sense of participation in a continuing process.

The United Nations men work on the topmost scaffolding of the historical structure, laying the highest courses that have yet been added to its masonry. It is a dizzy job, on which a workman may well break his neck, but the very fact that it is perilous is a guaranty that it is not tedious.

The craftsmen are bound to be conscious of the fact that the thing may collapse under them, as the League of Nations collapsed; but they are also aware that if what they are building does stand, to future generations it will seem to soar, and posterity will look back with awe on the men who constructed it.

In brief, it is putative accomplishment, and the mere chance of genuine accomplishment adds to the dimensions of one's existence, satisfies the urge of *Homo faber*, Man the Maker, which is certainly as powerful as that of *Homo sapiens*, Man the Knower. But to call this idealistic is questionable. Idealism, as most of us understand it, is conformity, usually involving some sacrifice, to a consciously formulated code; but the drive that impels *Homo faber* is instinctual. It follows that the energy of those leaders whom we admire is an exceptionally high concentration of a force that, diluted, is present in all of us; there is a trace of the United Nations man in you, in me, and in Joe Doakes down the street.

Are we three monstrous? To say that the basic idea of the United Nations is contrary to human nature implies as much; for the basic idea is construction, identical with the impulse that leads one man to build a chicken coop and another to build a cathedral. The difference is merely the greater difficulty that attends the construction of a world order. That difficulty has defeated all efforts from the time of Alexander the Great up to the time of John F. Kennedy. But the transmutation of elements defeated all efforts for thousands of years, yet it was not impossible. After the passage of ages, when alchemy at last became chemistry, the thing was done, and the prospect is that henceforth it will be done with increasing ease. The alchemists simply did not know enough about their own art.

The counsel of despair is that this analogy is utterly false because the development of alchemy into chemistry can never be paralleled by a development of politics into polity, certainly not in a democracy, because *demos* is simply not up to it. But why not? *Demos*, atomized, is *Homo faber*, who, in his scientific capacity, performed the impossibility of the transmutation of elements; where is the proof that in his social capacity he loses the impulse and the ingenuity to fabricate? Naturally the event is not to be predated, like Milne's dream of peace, "say, starting on Saturday week," but to assert that it will never be done is to revert to the error of the scoffers of the Middle Ages who *knew* that the alchemists' dream was pure nonsense.

This is, I admit, but cold comfort to Dr. Graham, Mr. Stevenson, and other harried and harassed gentlemen, whether from Chicago or Xanadu, as they patiently lay stone upon stone amid the slings and arrows of the scornful. I cannot comfort them, for I don't know what they are doing; any day the whole thing may fall down and bury them under the rubble, as their predecessors were buried. But if so, the site will be cleared, and *Homo faber* will start building again. I believe, furthermore, that unless the species is destroyed in some suicidal war, some among their successors will erect a political structure of a type that, to our present feeble imaginations, seems no less fabulous than Camelot, city of the Blameless King, or the capital of Prester John.

Trial Balance

"NO MAN IS AN ISLAND . . ." UH-HUH—AND ALL
things are relative, to and including the sermonizing of the
Rev. John Donne, which is true only as viewed from the
point to which it relates. From the opposite side it is quite
as clear that every man is an island, surrounded and cut off
by cold, gray seas of loneliness. Ask not for whom the bell
tolls, for all I know is that as long as I hear it, it does not
toll for me.

It is characteristic of the modern temper at once to
emphasize and disparage this disjunction. The public prints
are loaded with expatiations on the failure of communication, to which are attributed half the ills of our time, ranging
from the Cold War to the exclusion of the American chicken
from the European Common Market. This comes precisely
at the moment when the two great triumphs of science are,
on the one hand, the splitting of the atom and, on the other,
a forced conjunction that transmutes hydrogen into helium.
Either process results in a cataclysm of apocalyptic magnitude. You're damned if you do, and you're damned if you
don't.

There is pathos in this. That is undeniable, but it is also
immaterial; what is to the point is to recognize the reality
of the dilemma. Civilization could be detonated either by
a complete failure of communication or by its too complete

success. The fierce, white light of instantaneous transmission of information could, theoretically, reveal to others our hidden charms; but in practice it is more likely to reveal our warts, wens, scars, and deformities that should have remained covered for decency's sake.

In the late summer of 1963 a Christian church in Birmingham, Alabama, was desecrated by the blood of four little girls, murdered within the sacred precincts, not in a religious war, but as a result of a squabble among grown men over civil, which is to say political, rights. Within twenty-four hours the newspapers of Bangkok were giving their readers detailed accounts of the human sacrifice on the altar of Alabama politics. There was no failure of communication in that case. It was far too perfect for our comfort.

True, in that instance it was not the communication that blackened the face of America, it was the crime; but it is only too easy to cite cases in which the communication itself is a crime, and then, of course, the more perfect the communication, the more heinous the offense. When a lie is communicated we have cause to lament the energy and ingenuity of our technicians.

Surely, no American will deny that the Declaration of Independence is part of the footing of the piers that support our political structure; but the men who issued the Declaration did so "appealing to the Supreme Judge of the world for the rectitude of our intentions." They called God to witness, the most solemn of oaths in civil or canon law. When and if this formula becomes a mere habit of speech, empty of significant content, our modern structure is certainly not in line with the foundation and may be leaning dangerously out of plumb.

Since war is the summation of all evil, it is logical enough that it should be the great teacher of mendacity. So when a nation has been at war pretty constantly for fifty years—

counting from the first clash with Mexico in 1913, and re-
membering Haiti, Nicaragua, Santo Domingo, China, and
the other pestiferous small wars that punctuated the inter-
vals between the great ones—it is bound to have developed
not only skill in, but a corroding tolerance of, the art of lying.

When the first secret reports of the test explosion at Los
Alamos in 1945 reached Washington, Admiral Leahy, the
navy's chief expert on explosives, dismissed them as nonsense, because he was certain that the thing couldn't be
done. I am no expert on explosives, but when I read in the
newspapers on August 7, 1945, that we had produced an
explosion of unimaginable power over Hiroshima I was, like
Leahy, convinced that it was science fiction posing as war
propaganda; but when I saw that the announcement was a
direct quotation from Harry S. Truman, I believed against
all reason; for I deemed it still further beyond reason that
the President of the United States should issue a public statement that was a flat, direct lie. He might conceal the truth,
yes. He might evade it. He might issue, as many Presidents
had issued, statements that put the truth in such a light that
many people would deceive themselves. But the lie direct—
well, that simply was not done by the Chief Magistrate, the
successor of George Washington. Therefore I had to believe
in the atom bomb.

But since the U-2 incident, soon followed by the Bay
of Pigs incident, I have not rejoiced in any such certainty.
I am not prepared to assert that either President Eisenhower
or President Kennedy knew at the moment he issued it that
his statement was false. I suspect that each had been given
false information by his subordinates. Nevertheless, in each
instance the Presidency was smeared by a lie—and nobody
was hanged for it!

If discovery of the lie had been followed in each case by
a furious purge in the White House, the error might have

been partially retrieved. But there was no purge and there was no strong public demand that heads should roll. President and people alike, we took it in stride; and this toleration of perjury on the highest levels is a new development, indicative of a slackening of the people's regard for the highest office.

It is my belief, based on a wide, if unsystematic, reading of history that any slackening of the standard of probity applied to men in high office weakens the fabric of any political system and is doubly dangerous in a democratic system. The foundation of democracy is a presumption of good faith; if it be granted that a high official may lie to the people, the whole master-and-servant relation is reversed, for no servant may with impunity lie to his master. If an official may lie to the people, then he is the master and they are the servants.

This tolerance is usually excused on the ground of military necessity, and the excuse may be valid. If so, it reinforces the argument that war is always destructive of democracy, if not by physical conquest, then by moral erosion. Many years ago Al Smith observed that in time of war "we adjourn the Constitution." Quite so. We do more than that—we also adjourn the Ten Commandments, including "Thou shalt not bear false witness."

Political freedom is not consonant with war. That is all there is to it. When a nation has been pretty constantly at war for half a century, freedom in that country is bound to be impaired and it is idle to expect a high moral tone in the conduct of its public affairs.

In 1963 there was a tremendous furor in this country over civil rights, to the almost total neglect of civil liberties. The right of a Negro to eat in any public restaurant was sedulously protected, but not his right to express the opinion that lying, stealing, and murder as government policies are really unseemly. The expression of any such opinion is liable to bring him before the Un-American Activities Committee. There is nothing illogical in this when one reflects that modern war can be conducted successfully only by a coalition of militarists and industrialists, whose concern for civil liberties takes no high priority. Even Eisenhower, himself a soldier for forty years, eventually waked up to this. Just before his retirement from the White House he issued a warning, largely ignored by his countrymen, against domination of the country by a clique of high-ranking officers and great industrialists—by the users and producers of munitions. Yet the retiring President was perfectly correct; any group given the use of fifty billions a year is dangerously powerful. A similar combination destroyed Japan, and there is little reason to doubt that it could lead us to our destruction.

But will it? Not necessarily. If the affairs of men were governed by Aristotelian logic there would be no doubt about it. More than fifty years ago—that is to say, before the cycle of wars began—Henry Adams demonstrated with impeccable logic that the end was inevitable and probably close at hand, basing his conclusion on the relatively innocuous invention of the dynamo. But the progression of events has not followed Adams' thinking any more than it has followed Marx's. This prevalence of illogic maddens the learned doctors, but it is encouraging and even charming to simple minds.

Morally and intellectually we are the worse for all the fighting we have done since this century began; but that we are fatally injured is not yet proved.

On November 22, 1963, the President of the United States was assassinated, an occurrence that reduced to triviality, as far as popular interest is concerned, every other event of 1963 in the field of public affairs. On that date the manuscript of the rest of this book was already in the hands of the printer. Yet to publish comment on the events of 1963 without mentioning the tragedy at Dallas would be worse than an absurdity; it would be omission of the clinching argument sustaining the main thesis of this work.

The emotional response of the country to the crime was in great measure only what was to be expected of any civilized people—horror, grief, wrath, and shame. But there was another emotional factor, widespread yet not to be expected, and possibly more significant than any of the to-be-taken-for-granted emotions. This was simple astonishment. Americans of every region, every party, every faction, asked themselves and one another, "Why Kennedy, of all people?"

John Fitzgerald Kennedy had opponents, naturally, but they were opponents of his policies. There was, of course, the inevitable lunatic fringe that knows no method of political opposition other than personal vituperation. On the morning of the President's arrival in the Texas city, a Dallas newspaper published, as a paid advertisement, a series of questions addressed to Mr. Kennedy. They were studiedly insolent and pejorative, and their publication at the moment when the President was the city's guest, especially their publication for money, was a municipal disgrace that Dallas will not soon live down. But there is no evidence that the newspaper that published or the people who paid for the insult had any connection with the assassin.

At first there were various assumed connections. Indeed, half the country, on hearing the news, promptly assumed that the murderer was an agent of the reaction typified by the John Birch Society, while the other half assumed that he must be an agent of the Soviet Union. The failure of all efforts to trace a connection with either left public opinion confused, for vast numbers, probably a majority of the American people, could not imagine any other motive. Hence the widespread astonishment.

Yet there is another motive, without doubt involving insanity, yet capable of coherent, even rational analysis, and perfectly comprehensible in the light of the past history of the criminal. All the evidence indicates that the deed was done by a man named Oswald. Unfortunately, police negligence allowed Oswald himself to be killed before the facts could be examined in a court of law, with the result that though the President has appointed a commission to investigate the case, his guilt is sure to be the subject of popular argument for many years to come. Still there is no reasonable doubt that Oswald did it.

Whether he was a madman in the legal sense can never be known; but it is immaterial, for public opinion has always had but slight esteem for the legal definition of the term. In the opinion, and parlance, of laymen, he was as crazy as a loon. The opinion is based on these established facts: (a) Oswald had never met or communicated with Kennedy, so could have had no personal animus against him; (b) Kennedy was President of the United States and, as such, entitled to the respect of every sane American; (c) while the President had political opposition, personally he was the very model of a popular idol, young, brave, handsome, and highhearted, the sort of leader whom the people have always adored; (d) Oswald's wife said that he confessed having tried to kill Major General Edwin A. Walker, politically the very antithesis of Kennedy. How, asks the layman, can these contradictions be accounted for save on the theory that the man was the wildest of lunatics?

At the moment when he pulled the trigger doubtless he was a homicidal maniac; but the question then arises, how did he get that way? Even the psychiatrists admit that psychoses of this kind are progressive and are readily accelerated by an unfavorable environment. Subsequent investigation has shown that Oswald was what is known technically as a frustrated personality, and non-technically as a born fall guy. We have all known the type—the kind of man who seems to be licked from the start, who is slapped down every time he tries to stand up. It is not at all necessary that he should be pursued by vindictive, implacable personal enemies—circumstances are against him, he is unable to cope with the complexities of modern life, and he is whipped even when no man has laid a finger on him.

Relatively few of these go clean over the edge of madness and commit homicide, but they are uncomfortable people to have around. Thoroughly frustrated men and women hate the whole world, and they can give the world trouble, great trouble, short of murdering anybody, and far short of assassinating the head of the state. Large numbers of frustrated people are a threat to the social order, even though they may never produce an Oswald.

This is what gives a sinister tinge to the astonishment of the American people when President Kennedy was murdered. The astonishment is indicative of a dangerous ossification of opinion. Aside from Mr. Kennedy's personal attributes—although they appealed strongly to most of the nation—what he symbolized as President commands, alike through reason and through emotion, the deepest loyalty of most of us. We cannot quite believe, although we should know, that this response is less than unanimous, and when such an event as the assassination proves that it is not so we are amazed.

We are the more confused when we find it difficult to classify the crime against Kennedy. Four Presidents have been killed in office, and abortive attempts were made on two others, but the first five attacks fall into two categories. The murders of Lincoln and McKinley were definitely political, in the sense that they resulted from the impact of alien ideologies on unstable minds. The murder of Garfield was the revenge of a disappointed office seeker, that is to say, the venting of personal spite. So was the attempt to kill Jackson, while the attempt on Truman was obviously political.

The histories of other nations, as well as of our own, have made us familiar with personal hatred and political fanaticism as two causes of assassination. Personal enmity may arise from so many causes that it is unpredictable; but it did not figure in this case, so it may be dismissed. It is generally believed, however, that Czolgosz would not have killed a radical President or Booth a reactionary one.

Here, though, we have a man who shot President Kennedy and shot at General Walker. It is not of record that he had any personal contact with either man, so the inescapable inference is that he hated, not the individuals, but what they stood for. Kennedy was rated as a liberal, Walker as an extreme reactionary; the one thing they had in common was that both had worn the uniform of the United States, while Kennedy, as President, was the living symbol of the country. We cannot escape the disconcerting supposition that what Oswald hated was not the men, but the United States of America, as each, in his different way, represented the government. It seems clear that in his distorted mind was the illusion that he was shooting, not at Walker-Kennedy, but at Uncle Sam.

Too many of us succumb to the temptation to dismiss this as a psychosis, strictly the concern of the medical profession and about which the layman has no obligation, or even a right to form an opinion. This is quite correct when the disorder goes to the extreme of inducing homicidal mania, and partially true when it incites the victim to anti-social conduct less heinous, but still illegal. There is, however, a very wide range between the assassin and the good citizen, and the gradations on that scale are innumerable. The point is that if conditions exist in this country that will drive an un-

stable mind into murderous frenzy, the same conditions will
produce in relatively stable minds an attitude that bodes the
state no good. If we develop in the United States an element
—of appreciable size as compared to the whole population—
that is filled with distrust and dislike of Americanism, the
prognosis, as the doctors say, is not favorable for the social
order. And this is very much the concern of laymen.

There is an ominously large body of evidence that this is
just what we are doing. The so-called "hard core" of the
unemployed fluctuates slightly, but in recent years has
tended to increase, and it is already in the order of four or
five millions. As Myrdal has pointed out, under existing conditions expansion of the economy will be accompanied by a
corresponding expansion of the hard core. Marx long ago
emphasized the danger of alienating a worker from his work,
that is, making the job dull routine in which a man can take
neither pride nor interest. But even Marx did not envisage
alienation of a worker, not from his job only, but from all
work. Yet in America we are facing the appalling condition
of having on our hands some millions of men who will never
work again because the economy as it is now organized
offers no demand for the kind of labor they are capable of
performing. They are frustrated men, almost totally frustrated; and while the effect may not be to convert them
into Oswalds, it may easily be to make them decidedly bad
eggs.

What that may mean was luridly illustrated in England
a hundred and fifty years ago in the Luddite riots, when the
technologically unemployed wrecked machines and burned
factories in a futile protest against automation. But the
parallel between that situation and ours is not exact. The
unemployment of those days was in fact strictly technological, and the advance of technology soon abated it; ours is
structural and, if Myrdal is right, expansion of the economy
will not abolish but increase it.

Automation is technical and the persons it displaces are chiefly craftsmen and technicians, men of intelligence, certainly, but with an intellectual capacity ranging from the median downward oftener than upward. Ned Ludd, prototype of the English rioters, was by general agreement half-witted, and his imitators, while better than that, were certainly not drawn from the intellectual élite. Policemen's clubs and a few bayonets rapidly subdued them, but there is very reason to suppose that with able leadership they would have been far more dangerous.

Our structural unemployment, however, is not purely technical, but to a significant extent scientific. Changes being introduced with increasing frequency are not new inventions, or improvements on existing methods and processes, but extensions of knowledge of basic principles. In modern industry not mere craftsmen and technicians, but managers on the highest policy-making level, face the necessity of learning a new mathematics and a new logic, from which, of course, there must evolve a new economics and eventually a new philosophy.

Consider the plight of an engineer who graduated from a first-rate school at the head of his class fifteen years ago and has since made a satisfactory, even a brilliant career in, for example, some branch of electronics. If that man is still a master of his own science he is exceptional. In nine cases out of ten last year's graduate of the same school knows more about electronics than the man who has climbed to the position of head of the department.

The corporation for which he works now faces the loss of one of two values. It must sacrifice the value of the man's administrative experience, or it must risk loss of its competitive position in the industry. The alternative is to take the older man off the job and send him back to school for at least a year's intensive study; for most of the new knowledge is too abstruse to be mastered in any less time. But the alternative is very expensive, and it would be a formidable task to justify the outlay to a typical board of directors.

Ideally, of course, the man would simply take a year's leave of absence and spend it and five thousand dollars of his own money at the Massachusetts Institute of Technology, or an equivalent thereof. But how many men of the Class of 1950, able, but not with the special ability of a Billie Sol Estes, have accumulated five thousand dollars and have *not* accumulated an expensive family in the last fifteen years? As usual, the ideal solution is seldom practical.

Far more frequent than the ideal is the compromise solution. The corporation discharges or downgrades the older man in order to protect its competitive position, which adds to the discontented one more partially or totally frustrated man. Unless he is a very strong character he will also become a partially or totally embittered man. But he will remain a brainy man, and he will not have lost the capacity for leadership that fifteen years' experience have developed. His ability and his training will be potentially available for any kind of enterprise.

What it comes to is that circumstances are furnishing competent officers to a great and increasing army of the permanently unemployed. Anyone who can view that situation complacently must have shut down his mental operations, if he had any mentality to begin with. Yet for years our self-appointed guardians of national security have roared up and down the land pursuing "outside agitators" and yelling about "infiltration," but paying no attention to local breeding grounds of native haters of the American system.

The explanation of this misdirected effort is simple enough. Structural unemployment cannot be attributed to any personal devil. Even the Un-American Activities Committees realize that you can't make people believe that any business tycoon, however ruthless, deliberately set out to eliminate customers from the market, so they are impelled to lay the blame on communism, or "creeping socialism," or some other alien influence. They cannot point to structural unemployment, because that is not only Made in U.S.A., but is the resultant of an extremely intricate combination of forces. To unravel it will require thought, probably long and intensive thinking, and our self-appointed guardians have never been conspicuous for their brainpower. For all their chatter about defending the American way of life, they do not know how to be free and have no great desire to learn; they are at one with the slave in ancient Rome who aspired, not to freedom, but to have a slave of his own whom he could beat every day. Unfortunately, among the victims they have chosen to belabor are some of the few relatively free spirits among us—Oppenheimer, Lattimore, Condon, for instance—while the more frantic among them have assailed even Eisenhower and Warren. Kennedy, of course, was a favorite target.

However, from the national, not the individual, standpoint, these idiots are nuisances rather than real threats to the survival of the republic. The clear and present danger is a steady increase in the proportion of frustrated and embittered people in the population, an increase that the presence of structural unemployment seems to guarantee. A remedy, of course, is philosophically possible, even if it is not at present visible. The economic system is a creation of the human mind, and whatever man can make, man can mend.

But it will not be done by the instrumentalities at present available. The three economic systems that now dominate the world, capitalism, socialism, and communism, are all glaringly inadequate. Something new is imperatively demanded. Hence the current disposition to equate innovation with high treason is not statecraft, it is suicidal mania.

As long as every suggestion of a re-examination of basic principles is penalized, by law or by public opinion, the prospect will remain grim.

Fortunately, there is historical evidence that, though it does not prove, does suggest that the contemporary hatred of anything resembling thought in politics is a passing phase. The removal of political bondage is the indispensable first step toward creating an environment in which men can learn how to be free. As a people we are certainly not masters of that knowledge, but we have produced individuals who have nearly, if not completely, mastered it. George Washington was a man who knew how to be free. Many hold that Benjamin Franklin was another. Jefferson, Jackson, Lincoln, Wilson, Roosevelt, were all caught in the toils of external circumstance and for a large part of the time acted under compulsion. But the fetters they wore were external. They were not chained by their own ignorance of the fact that freedom is a process, not a status.

What one man can do another can imitate, and there is no reason in law or in logic to set a limit to the number of Americans who may acquire the knowledge that will make them freemen *de facto* as well as *de jure*. But it isn't an operation in mass production; it is an individual enterprise, and the ruggedest individualism there is. Yet today, as in 1776, there are those who are trying it, and they will not be stopped because now and then one dies by violence in the attempt. Such a tragedy only sharpens their realization of how necessary is the effort. In measure as their number increases, so will multiply the republic's chances of purging itself of the seeds of death, to survive through a future beyond our capacity to measure.

> "Fight on, my men," Sir Andrew says,
> "A little I'm hurt, but yet not slain;
> I'll but lie down and bleed awhile,
> And then I'll rise and fight again,"

is poetry, not medical science, but poetry exists as surely
as science, and is a good deal older. It is highly probable,
too, that it has had more to do with the course of history,
no matter what the determinists say. Perhaps every modifi-
cation of the original design of Chartres Cathedral would
have maddened the architects if they had not been dead.
Perhaps the thing would have been a great deal finer if the
original design had been faithfully followed. Since we do not
have it, we cannot know. What we do know is that it is beau-
tiful and that it has stood for seven hundred years. What the
dead architects would say of it if they could see it today, I
do not know; but I think the dead hod-carriers would be
satisfied and glad that they had a hand in its building.

As one among those present during rather more than a
third of the construction, so far, of the American republic,
I choose to bet against Adams and Marx and on George
Bancroft. George was a bad historian, as the faculty has
abundantly proved, but it does not necessarily follow that
he was an equally bad prophet, for sometimes people arrive
at correct conclusions in spite of bad reasoning. Aesop's fly
on the axle of the rolling chariot that cried, "What a dust
I am raising!" was not deceived as to the dust. Bancroft's
conviction that the moral elevation of American political
principles made inevitable this nation's leadership of the
world is questionable, to put it mildly, but it does not follow that leadership of the world will not be attained and
retained for as much of the future as holds any interest for
the living generation.

To the rigid logician, liberty under law seems to be, and
may be in fact, a contradiction in terms. But an imperfect,
yet desirable liberty, under an imperfect, yet tolerable law
has been attained and exists—precariously, but definitely—
at this moment. The history of liberty in this country has
followed a zigzag course. At the moment it is at the bottom
of its worst dip since 1798, when panic inspired by the

Jacobins in Paris drove us almost to the extinction of liberty by the Alien and Sedition Laws.

Legally, indeed, we are below that point, for the Espionage Act of 1917—never repealed—plus the Smith Act, plus the McCarran Act, plus the various Un-American Activities Committees are far more destructive of political liberty than were the Alien and Sedition Acts. This is no cause for wonder since the panic inspired by the Communists in Moscow has been immensely greater and much longer-lasting than that inspired by the French Revolution. Furthermore, we have not produced this time a Jefferson strong enough to refute the philosophy of poltroonery and persuade us to run the risk of being free. That is to say, we have not produced one yet; but it is not for this observer to assume omniscience by announcing that none will or can be produced by the contemporary generation. It could be that American political liberty is on the verge of extinction; but it could be that it is on the verge of a magnificent comeback. Pay your money and take your choice.

My money is on Bancroft as a better prophet than Marx or Adams because I translate his categorical imperative into simple futurity. I harbor grave doubt that the United States has earned the right to lead the free world, but at this moment it is leading and it may very well lead for some time to come. There is also a distinct possibility that in the process of leading it may become fit to lead, and so hold the position for quite a long time.

The evidence in support of this cheerful view is, I must admit, wispy. It is merely the result of individual observation of the country's course over a period longer than the Psalmist thought a man has a right to live. It seems to me that the zigzag line from 1890 as far as 1963 tends to rise rather than sink. I think that as an American citizen I enjoy a somewhat wider liberty than was permitted to my father.

For emphasis I repeat—I think so. Other than Marx and Adams, many men, wiser than I, have said and are saying the contrary; but on the other hand, I enjoy the company of at least an equal number of men to whose wisdom I bow. Therefore I feel justified in taking the cheerful view, although not dogmatically.

In the year of my birth there were 127 lynchings in the United States, and two years later that form of outdoor sport reached the peak of its popularity, with 255 mob murders. All but a handful of the victims were Negroes, but civilized white southerners, such as my father, took real and serious risks in denouncing the practice. To that extent they were enslaved. By my time the risk of physical violence was negligible; it is the editor who refuses to denounce the mob who invites reprisals today.

In the year of my birth a Congress endowed with the courage of Little Miss Muffett allowed the self-appointed censor of morals, Anthony Comstock, to misuse the power of the government to block the development of literature and art in this country. Comstock, with the esthetic taste of a chimpanzee, yet had more nerve than the whole assemblage of politicos in Washington, and he continued to crack the whip over them until he died in 1915. At that it was the judiciary, not the legislative, that eventually struck off the fetters that Comstock had fastened on intellectual freedom.

I was four years old when Grover Cleveland used the United States Army to thrust labor into a state of peonage that lasted until Franklin D. Roosevelt ended it forty years later. Now the boot is on the other foot; thirty years after the Wagner Act, it is Big Labor that threatens to hold politics in thrall.

But why labor the point? Even at the nadir of civil liberties to which nervous old women—mostly of the masculine gender—have dragged us on account of their obsession that there is a Communist behind every bedpost, we are measurably closer to being freemen than we were in the closing decade of the nineteenth century.

If that is indeed the case, I am convinced that we owe it to an increasing awareness of the tentative nature of our experiment in self-government. That awareness is still confined to a minority, but the minority tends to enlarge and it will continue to enlarge as long as we retain even fragmentary freedom of opinion and freedom of expression. The only sound philosophy of American history is one that weighs accurately both the risks and the promises of freedom, aware that it is not yet attained, but hopeful that its attainment is closer than it ever has been before.

This presupposes, of course, that posterity will engender a sufficient number of better men than we are. Well, why not? No millennial dawnism is involved in the idea. The next generation may be not a whit improved morally and yet be more efficient intellectually than ours has been. For one thing, if history is being better written than it has been in the past—and I believe it is—the next generation will have better intellectual tools with which to further the construction of a political structure that will withstand the battering of time and chance as sturdily and as long as Chartres Cathedral has withstood them.

They will make their own errors, of course. Some of their work will be out of plumb and will fall down, as our Eighteenth Amendment fell down. Perhaps they will add as many grotesques and gargoyles as we have added and yet find that in the end they add piquancy without destroying the unity of the whole. And perhaps, just perhaps, they may generate supreme artists who will execute and set in place some rose window that will put to shame the finest work of medieval craftsmen.

I do not know that they will do this; but, I add without apology, you do not know that they will not. So I think that we who are passing may hand over our tools, which we must do anyhow, and in handing them over quote Hardy blithely:

> And ye, red-lipped and smooth-browed; list,
>   Gentlemen;
> Much there is waits you we have missed;
> Much lore we leave you worth the knowing,
> Much, much has lain outside our ken:
> Nay, rush not; time serves; we are going,
>   Gentlemen.